Gandhi and Nehru: Reflections Through Letters

Books by the Same Author

- Complete Biography of Mahatma Gandhi (The) (in 3 Volumes)
- Gandhi in Modern World
- Inspiring Thoughts of Mahatma Gandhi: Gandhi in Daily Life
- Mahatma Gandhi on Ethics
- Mahatma Gandhi on Sarvodaya
- Mahatma Gandhi on Untouchability
- Mahatma Gandhi Speaks: Selected Speeches and Writings
- Revisiting Hind Swaraj
- Understanding Gandhi: Speeches and Writings That Reveal His Mind, Methods and Mission
- World Crisis and the Gandhi Way
- Mahatma Gandhi on Health
- Gaol Experiences of Mahatma Gandhi

About the Author

Anil Dutta Mishra is a distinguished Gandhian Scholar and Writer. He started his career as Assistant Professor in the Department of Non-violence and Peace Studies, Jain Vishva Bharati University, Ladnun, Rajasthan, became Deputy Director of National Gandhi Museum and Honorary Professor, Centre for Gandhian Philosophy and Human Development, Gayatri Vidya Parishad Degree College [Autonomous], Visakhapatnam. Presently, he is treasure, IIPA, Delhi Regional Branch, New Delhi and Professor Research, UPRTOU, Allahabad.

Mishra has held the post of General Secretary of Indian Society of Gandhian Studies, Alliance for Sarvodaya, Member Board of Studies, Nagpur and Punjab Universities and is Member of Gandhian Studies Centre of different colleges and universities across India. He has authored/edited 30 books and published a number of research papers. His recent book **Reading Gandhi** is widely acclaimed.
E-mail: anilduttamishra@gmail.com

Gandhi and Nehru
Reflections Through Letters

Anil Dutta Mishra

CONCEPT PUBLISHING COMPANY PVT. LTD.
NEW DELHI-110059

ISBN-13: 978-93-5125-266-5

First Published 2017

Published and Printed by

Concept
Since 1974

Concept Publishing Company Pvt. Ltd.
Regd. Office:
A/15-16, Commercial Block, Mohan Garden,
New Delhi-110059 (INDIA)
Phones : 25351460, 25351794, *Fax* : 091-11-25357109
Email : publishing@conceptpub.com
Website: www.conceptpub.com

Editorial Office: H-13, Bali Nagar, New Delhi-110 015, India.

Cataloging in Publication Data—DK Courtesy: D.K. Agencies (P) Ltd. <docinfo@dkagencies.com>

Gandhi, *Mahatma,* 1869-1948.
[Correspondence. Selections]
Gandhi and Nehru : reflections through letters / [edited by] Anil Dutta Mishra.
pages cm
Includes bibliographical references and indexes.
ISBN 9789351252665

1. Gandhi, Mahatma, 1869-1948—Correspondence. 2. Nehru, Jawaharlal, 1889-1964—Correspondence. 3. Statesmen—India—Correspondence. 4. India—Politics and government—1919-1947. 5. India—History—20th century. I. Mishra, Anil Dutta, 1965- editor. II. Nehru, Jawaharlal, 1889-1964. Correspondence. Selections. III. Title.

DS481.G3G36 2017 DDC 954.035 23

Preface

Mahatma Gandhi and Pandit Jawaharlal Nehru shaped the distiny of India and Indians. One cannot think of India without Bapu and Chacha Nehru. They became natural leader of India by sheer of hard work, honesty, prestine purity, always ready to work for the motherland and its people and set example for others to follow. They were iconic personalities. They derived legacy through their creativeness, thought, action and deed. Gandhi said that my life is message. Similarly, for Nehru: *Aram is Haram*.

In pre-Independence India Gandhi dominated the freedom struggle being a undisputed leader. Contrary, in post-Independent India Nehru being a first Prime Minister built everything from scratch. Jawaharlal Nehru built brick by brick India and laid strong foundation of strong Parliamentary democracy and all modern institutions and system of governance. Today we are calling ourself proudly that India is self-sufficient in food, vivrant democracy, secular and emerging super power. We are nuclear power, space power and what not. Credit goes to Pandit Jawaharlal Nehru and his Cabinet colleagues.

Sacrifice of Gandhi and Nehru for the cause of country and people was un-parallel in Indian history. We can criticise, romanticised Gandhi and Nehru which is natural due to idealogical differences. But, we must remember that we cannot afford to ignore their sacrifice and contribution. Gandhi and Nehru must be seen in Text and Context. They were close associates and derived strength from each other. They were responding to contemporary challenges but its impact was everlasting. India was in their blood. They dedicated their lives for her liberation. One can see Nehru in Gandhi and Gandhi in Nehru.

Gandhi and Nehru met for the first time during Lucknow Congress during Christmas 1916. In due course of time, Nehru became a true follower of Gandhi. Not a blind one. Nehru wrote about Gandhi in An Autobiography—"What a wonderful man was Gandhiji after all, with his amazing and almost irresistible charm and subtle power over people. His writings and his sayings conveyed little enough impression of the man behind; his personality was far bigger than they would lead one to think. And his service to India, how vast they had been. He had instilled courage and manhood in her people, and discipline and endurance, and the power of joyful sacrifice for a cause, and, with all his humility, pride. Courage is the one sure foundation of character, he had said; without courage there is no morality, no religion, no love. "One cannot follow truth or love so long as one is subject to fear." With all his horror of violence, he had told us that "cowardice is a thing even more hateful than violence." And "discipline is the pledge and guarantee that a man means business. There is no deliverance and no hope without sacrifice, discipline, and self-control. Mere sacrifice without discipline will be unavailing. Words only and pious phrases perhaps, rather platudinous, but there was power behind the words, and India knew that this little man meant business."

Further Nehru wrote: "He came to represent India to an amazing degree and to express the very spirit of that ancient and tortured land. Almost he was India, and his very failings were Indian failings. A slight to him was hardly a personal matter, it was an insult to the nation..."

Nehru himself admitted in *The Discovery of India* that "Some kind of ethical approach to life has a strong appeal for me, though it would be difficult for me to justify logically. I have been attracted by Gandhiji's stress on right means and I think one of his greatest contributions to our public life has been this emphasis. The idea is by no means new, but this application of an ethical doctrine to large-scale public activity was certainly novel. It is full of difficulty, and perhaps ends and means are not really separable but from together one organic whole."

Gandhi and Nehru share a rare bond of love, affection and understanding of each other thought and action. To understand Gandhi and Nehru we have to be objective and analytical but at the same time synergic, interdisciplinary, and holistic. Unfortunately, we are trained to be specialists; we see the parts but not the whole. But if everything is related to everything else, and nothing stands apart, knowing the part alone would lead to knowing the whole. Universe is a system of which the solar system is a sub-system; in the solar system, the earth is sub-system; in the earth as a system, lithosphere, hydrosphere, ionosphere, atmosphere and biosphere are sub-systems; in the biosphere, human species form a sub-system; in the human species each family and individual forms a sub-system. This being the case, to understand even an individual in full, we have to treat his as a part of the whole universe. True he is more closely related to the systems nearer him but he is influenced and he influences by his thoughts and deeds not only his fellow human beings, but also all that surrounds him, nature included. All that we do has its implication far wider than we realize. Real Gandhi and Nehru is a systems man and unless we see him that way, we cannot understand him.

Firstly, Gandhi and Nehru both have firm faith in freedom and democratic values. Secondly, Gandhi and Nehru both studied in England and having liberal outlook. Gandhi spent 21 years in South Africa. Which give him experience how to fight non-violently with mighty British Empire. Gandhi and Nehru widely travelled and long stay in England have direct impact on Gandhi and Nehru thinking. Thirdly, Gandhi and Nehru by birth they are Hindu. But they are secular in public and private life. Fourthly, Gandhi and Nehru never lived a life of duality. They never have any mask. Internally and externally they are *karmayogi*. Fifthly, Gandhi and Nehru both have deep understanding of Indian History, Civilization and Culture. Gandhi look ancient wisdom in modern context. He wrote *Indian Home Rule* or *Hind Swaraj*, *An Autobiography* or *My Experiment With Truth* and *Satyagraha in South Africa*. These three books are essential to understand Gandhi. Similarly, Jawaharlal Nehru's three classic—*Glimpses of World History*, *An Autobiography* and *The Discovery of India*—remain essential reading for understanding his ideas. Finally, both derived power from masses. They inspired masses and mass inspired them. They connect themselves with masses. They became their natural leader. Both will be remember forever till India exists.

Gandhi had a firm faith that Jawaharlal will speak when Gandhi was no more. After going through words and deeds of Nehru one can draw a conclusion that in every sense Nehru was a true Gandhian. He had an idea of India and Indians. Whatever the fruit of development we are enjoying credit goes to Nehru. He laid the foundation of Modern India. We have today viverant democracy, independent Election Commission and Judiciary. Nehru gave us AIIMs, IITs, IIMs, Bhakra-Nangal Dam, Hirakud, BARC, Indian Space Programme, BHEL, Steel Plants and other industrial complexes which are essential for development of newly Independent country like India. We, the educated people and Gandhians, who are basically anti-Gandhi in their thought, action and deed, create a watertight compartment between Gandhi and Nehru. One must read Nehru's first speech which he gave after geting freedom from the yoke of British Empire. Every word carry meaning and vision for future what he wanted to do for India and Indians. Nehru fulfil the dream of Bapu. Methods may be different but every action of Nehru was Gandhian keeping the aspiration of people of newly Independent country. Gandhi rightly said about Nehru on April 1, 1947 at Prayer meeting that "By the grace of God, we have a gem of man in our midst who wants to embrace the whole world. Should we not maintain peace if only to honour him?" One can see Gandhi in Nehru and Nehru in Gandhi.

Gandhi used to write letters to Jawahar. Similarly, Jawahar used to write to Gandhi. Whatever letters I got in *The Collected Works of Mahatma Gandhi* are reproduced here without any distortions and alterations so that the readers drew their own conclusions. These letters are treasure of information and function like a lighthouse in the journey of thought in the ocean of knowledge. These letters are chronologically arranged to enable the reader to understand Gandhi and Nehru and their relationship. The purpose of this book is to understand the two unique personalities of Modern India, Gandhi and Nehru, through their writings without any distortation. To make the book reader friendly it has been divided into two parts. In part one, all the letters written by Gandhi to Jawaharlal put Chronologically. In part two, Nehru's original letters are placed for reader's deeper understanding of the relationship of two great leaders. I am sure and hopeful that the book "*Gandhi and Nehru: Reflections Through Letters*" will open new vistas of research and proper understanding of Gandhi's relationship with Jawaharlal Nehru.

Today, we have forgetten Gandhi and Nehru. They stood for self-respect, honesty, integrity and self-esteem of individual and in system of governance. My lifelong mission is to promote Gandhian and Nehruvian values in individual, society, nation and whole world. I have no resources at my disposal. So, I decided to re-explore Gandhi's writing in modern context without taking any help from anywhere. By doing this I want to show the Gandhian and Gandhian Institutions what they are doing by receiving enormous funds from Government of India and State Governments and public. It is a wastage of hard earned tax paid money of people. They teach immorality in the name of morality. The Gandhian institutions are centre of anti-Gandhian and anti-national activities. They wear *Khadi* which is made of yarn of exploitation, criminality, casteism, regionalism and self-interest. *Khadi* is not mere a cloth but mission. Gandhians only preach never practice. They are hungry for grabing post by any means. They live luxurious life at public cost and too without contributing anything for society. *Kanchan* and *Kamani* are their *dharma*. They proclaimed themselves Gandhian leaders but without any followers. Gandhi got killed physically once but these so-called Gandhian are killing Gandhi's soul, sprit and core of his fundamental thought on which Gandhism is stand for. Gandhian's waste their time and energy in criticising Congress. The fact is that they have forgetten Gandhi. These are some hard facts. Contrarily, Gandhi is coming to us in form of Arab Spring and Anna Movement.

I am sure the book '*Gandhi and Nehru: Reflections Through Letters*' will open new vistas of research and proper understanding of Gandhi and Nehru.

In writing this book I had received, over the years, very valuable help from friends, teachers and colleagues. I am grateful to them. My family has always stood behind me in all my academic endeavours. My wife Dr. Sweta Mishra went through the final draft and provided her valuable inputs and insight.

Last but not the least, I am grateful to Shri Ashok Kumar Mittal of Concept Publishing Company Pvt. Ltd., for bringing out this book in present form and that too within record time.

Anil Dutta Mishra
anilduttamishra@gmail.com

Contents

PART ONE
Mahatma Gandhi's Letters to Jawaharlal Nehru

1. Letter to Jawaharlal Nehru

Sabarmati,
July 27, 1924

My Dear Jawaharlal,

In my opinion, you should enter into correspondence with the Government and ascertain the reason for the prohibition and say that, if anything can be pointed out to the committee as really objectionable, your committee would be prepared to delete the passages. If the Government return an unsatisfactory reply, you should intimate to them that the words will not be withdrawn from circulation.

The Government are not likely to bother the children and, even if they do, the only thing they can do is to remove the books from the children. The latter may be advised then not to mind and hand over the books to the police. I do not think there is any other penalty.

Please look up the law and let me know. I feel that no matter how much we may have become demoralized, we may not shirk a battle that may be given to us. We need not take up aggressive civil disobedience, we may not take up mass civil disobedience; but we must face that which comes our way and tests us. Don't you think so? How to give battle will be a question for you to decide as the situation develops.

Yours sincerely,
M. K. Gandhi

[PS.]
Pray do not worry about my health. It is all right and answers my purpose. You must be resourceful enough to mend the *charkha*.

For the handle all you need is an iron inset. Wood always non-co-operates with iron and gives in. Immediately you fix in an iron ring, you will find it will work all right. Please note that mere nails will not do. No part of the handle should have friction with the iron axle.

Yours,
M. K. G.

2. Letter to Jawaharlal Nehru[1]

September 15, 1924

My Dear Jawaharlal,

I have your most touching personal letter. You will stand it all bravely I know. Father is just now in an irritable mood. And I am most anxious that neither you nor I should contribute an iota to the irritation. If it is at all possible you should have a frank chat with him and avoid such action as may offend him. It makes me unhappy to find him unhappy. His irritability is a sure sign of his unhappiness.

Hasrat was here today and I find from him that even my proposal about spinning by every Congressman ruffles him. I do so feel like retiring from the Congress and doing the three things quietly. They are enough to occupy more than all the true men and women we can get. But even that ruffles people. I had a long chat with the *Poona Swarajists*. They will not agree to spin and they will not agree to my leaving the Congress. They do not realize that I shall cease to be useful as soon as I cease to be myself. It is a wretched situation but I do not despair. My faith is in God. I know only the moment's duty. It is given to me to know no more. Why then should I worry? Shall I try to arrange for some money for you? Why may you not take up remunerative work? After all you must live by the sweat of your brow even though you may be under Father's roof. Will you be correspondent to some newspapers? Or will you take up a professorship?

Yours sincerely,
M. K. Gandhi

---

1. Regarding this Jawaharlal Nehru wrote: "I had written to Gandhiji and said that I was rather unhappy to be a financial burden on my father and wanted to stand on my own feet. The difficulty was that I was a whole-time worker of the Congress. My father, when he heard of this, was greatly annoyed."

3. Letter to Jawaharlal Nehru

September 19, 1924

My Dear Jawaharlal,

You must not be stunned. Rather rejoice that God gives strength and direction to do my duty. I could not do otherwise. As the author of non-co-operation, a heavy responsibility lies on my shoulders. Do give me in writing your impressions of Lucknow and Cawnpore. Let me drink the cup to the full. I am quite at peace with myself.

Yours sincerely,
M. K. Gandhi

---

4. Letter to Jawaharlal Nehru

Delhi,
November 12, 1924

My Dear Jawaharlal,

It does appear to me to be necessary to have a flying column of workers, Hindu and Mohammedan, who would on a moment's notice be ready to go to afflicted parts for investigation. We may not wait always for distinguished men to go. Take for instance the case sent to you yesterday. If the statements made are true, the culprits should be exposed. If they are false, newspaper reporters should be brought to book. The investigation should be prompt and thorough. I am preparing Mahadev for the work and am trying to induce Pyarelal.

The latter is unnecessarily diffident. Will Manzar Ali do the work? He may be paid for it? He should have no objection to accepting remuneration. His spinning work need not be disturbed. His activity may be confined to U.P. only, though I would prefer not to have any restrictions unless we get an army of workers in the field. For the case sent to you yesterday, I hope you will send someone at once. What about the case that was sent to you some weeks ago?

Yours sincerely,
M. K. Gandhi

[PS.]

I take it you will be in Bombay with Father on Thursday morning if not earlier. I reach there that morning. Mrs. Naidu is leaving here tomorrow morning.

M. K. G.

5. Letter to Jawaharial Nehru

November 16, 1924

My Dear Jawaharlal,

Just a line to wish you many happy returns of the day for the service of the motherland and for self-realization.

If it is possible, do come with Father.

Yours sincerely,
M. K. Gandhi

---

6. Letter to Jawaharlal Nehru

Magh Sud 6, December 2, 1924

Dear Jawaharlal,

I have written something in *Young India*[1] about the textbooks of Prof. Ramdas Gaur. So I am not replying separately. I hope Kamala is well. I am going to the Punjab.

Blessings from
Mohandas Gandhi

Pandit Jawaharlal Nehru
Anand Bhavan
Allahabad

---

1. *Vide* "What is Seditious?", 4-12-1924.

7. Letter to Jawaharlal Nehru

April 25, 1925

My Dear Jawaharlal,

I am in Tithal, a place somewhat like Juhu, resting for four days to fit myself for the Bengal ordeal. I am trying here to overtake my correspondence in which I find your letter referring to the article "God and Congress".[1] I sympathize with you in your difficulties.

True religion being the greatest thing in life and in the world, it has been exploited the most. And those who have seen the exploiters and the exploitation and missed the reality naturally get disgusted with the thing itself. But religion is, after all, a matter for each individual, and then too a matter of the heart, call it then by whatever name you like, that which gives one the greatest solace in the midst of the severest fire is God. Anyway, you are on the right track. I do not mind reason being the sole test even though it often bewilders one and lands one in errors that border on superstition. Cow-protection to me is infinitely more than mere protection of the cow. The cow is merely a type for all that lives. Cow-protection means protection of the weak, the helpless, the dumb and the deaf. Man becomes then not the lord and master of all creation but he is its servant. The cow to me is a sermon on pity. As yet we are merely playing at cow-protection . But we shall soon have to grapple with the reality.

I hope you have received all my previous letters. I have a doleful letter from Mr. Satyapal[2]. I wish you could go to the Punjab even if it is only for a few days. Your visit will hearten him.

I wish Father would have two months in a quiet and cool place. And why will you not go to Almora for a week or so and combine work with a breath of cool air?

Yours,
Bapu

1. Dated March 3, 1925.
2. A medical practitioner and Congress leader of the Punjab.

8. Letter to Jawaharlal Nehru

Ashram,
Sabarmati,
April 23, 1926

My Dear Jawaharlal,

I have been thinking of writing to you every week and every week I have failed. I must not let this week, however, pass by. I have had the latest news about you from Father while he was here with the Responsivists. You will have seen the agreement[1] that has been arrived at.

Hindus and Muslims are going more and more away from each other. But this thing does not disturb me. Somehow or other, I feel that the separation is growing in order only to bring them all closer later on.

I do hope Kamala is benefiting.

Yours,
Bapu

1. *Vide* Appedndix "The Sabarmati Pact", April and May, 1926.

9. Letter to Jawaharlal Nehru[1]

Not Revised Satyagraha Ashram,
Sabarmati,
January 4, 1928

My Dear Jawaharlal,

I feel that you love me too well to resent what I am about to write. In any case I love you too well to restrain my pen when I feel I must write.

You are going too fast. You should have taken time to think and become acclimatized. Most of the resolutions you framed and got carried could have been delayed for one year. Your plunging into the 'republican army' was a hasty step. But I do not mind these acts of yours so much as I mind your encouraging mischief-makers and hooligans. I do not know whether you still believe in unadulterated non-violence. But even if you have altered your views, you could not think that unlicensed and unbridled violence is going to deliver the country. If careful observation of the country in the light of your European experiences convinces you of the error of the current ways and means, by all means enforce your own views, but do please from a disciplined party. You know the Cawnpore experiences. In every struggle bands of men who would submit to discipline are needed.

You seem to be overlooking this factor in being careless about your instruments.

If I can advise you, now that you are the working secretary of the Indian National Congress, it is your duty to devote your whole energy to the central resolution, i.e., Unity, and the important but secondary resolution, i.e., boycott of the Simon Commission.[2] The Unity resolution[3] requires the use of all you great gifts of organization and persuasion.

I have not time to elaborate my points, but *verb. sap.*

I hope Kamala is keeping as well as in Europe.

Yours,
Bapu

---

1. This was published along with the following note from Jawaharlal Nehru: "I returned from Europe in December 1927 and went straight to the Madras Session of the Indian National Congress. A number of resolutions were passed there at my instance. This letter was written by Gandhiji because he did not approve of some of my activities at this session."
2. *Vide* Appendix "Extract from Statement by the Viceroy on the Indian Statutory Commission", November 8, 1927.
3. *Vide* Appendix "Resolution on Hindu-Muslim Unity", December 26, 1927.

---

10. Letter to Jawaharlal Nehru

Satyagraha Ashram,
Sabarmati,
January 11, 1928

My Dear Jawaharlal,

I hope Chand[1] is out of the wood.

My point[2] is not that you had not thought out any of your resolutions, much less the Independence one; but my point is that neither you nor anyone else had thought out the whole situation and considered the bearing and propriety of the resolutions. The finest resolutions may be irrelevant or out of place. But you should read carefully my article on the Congress. The special article on Independence will be out tomorrow.

The Unity resolution need much working out.

Do come whenever you can and when you come bring your work here and give yourself enough time.

This is scrappy but can't give you more just now.

Yours,
Bapu

---

1. Eldest daughter of Vijayalakshmi Pandit.
2. *Vide* "Letter to Jawaharlal Nehru", 4-1-1928.

---

11. Letter to Jawaharlal Nehru[1]

Satyagraha Ashram,
Sabarmati,
January 15, 1928

My Dear Jawaharlal,

I have your letter which I appreciate more than anything else you could have written to me, because you are absolutely frank and I am glad for having written that article if only to draw from you what you have been keeping to ourself fall these long years. But of this later.

This I am dictating merely to tell you that poor Brockway is in a bad way. I understand that he will have to undergo another operation of a far more serious nature and might have to stay in India for many more months. I understand too that he has come with an understanding with the A.I.C.C. arrived at by Father that his passage to and fro should be paid by the Congress. If that is so, I suppose we should defray his hospital expenses also and perhaps these in any case seeing that he was coming to the Congress. I understand that he will be soon in arrears about his hospital charges. Will you please inquire and do the needful, even set the wire in motion if necessary.

I understand that the Madras Comittee has already paid nearly Rs. 400. The hospital charges alone are said to amount to Rs. 12 per day. I am writing to Srinivasa Iyengar also.

Yours sincerely,
Bapu

---

1. This letter in referred to in "Letter to Jawaharlal Nehru", 17-1-1928, as not available.

---

12. Letter to Jawaharlal Nehru[1]

The Ashram,
Sabarmati,
January 17, 1928

My Dear Jawaharlal,

I must dictate and save time and give rest to my aching shoulder. I wrote to you on Sunday about Fenner Brockway.[2] I hope you got that letter in due time.

Do you know that it was because you were the chief partner in the transactions referred to that I wrote the articles[3] you have criticized, except of course about the so-called 'All-India Exhibition'? I felt a kind of safety that, in view of the relations between you and me, my writings would be taken in the spirit in which they were written. However, I see that they were a misfire all-round. I do not mind it. For, it is evident that the articles alone could deliver you from the self-suppression under which you have been labouring apparently for so many years. Though I was beginning to detect some differences in viewpoint between you and me, I had no notion whatsoever of the terrible extent of these differences. Whilst you were heroically suppressing yourself for the sake of the nation and in the belief that by working with and under me in spite of yourself, you would serve the nation and come out scatheless, you were chafing under the burden of this unnatural self-suppression. And, while you were in that state, you overlooked the very things which appear to you now as my serious blemishes.

I could show you from the pages of *Young India* equally strong articles written by me, when I was actively guiding the Congress with reference to the doing of the All-India Congress Committee. I have spoken similarly at the All-India Congress Committee meetings whenever there has been irresponsible and hasty talk or action. But whilst you were under stupefaction these things did not jar on you as they do now. And it seems to me, therefore, useless to show you the discrepancies in your letter. What I am now concerned with is future action.

If any freedom is required from me, I give you all the freedom you may need from the humble, unquestioning allegiance that you have given to me for all these years and which I value all the more for the knowledge I have now gained of your state. I see quite clearly that you must carry on open warfare against me and my views. For, if I am wrong I am evidently doing irreparable harm to the country and it is your duty after having known it to rise in revolt against me. Or, if you have any doubt as to the correctness of your conclusion, I shall gladly discuss them with you personally. The differences between you and me appear to me to be so vast and radical that there seems to be no meeting-ground between us. I can't conceal from you my grief that I should lose a comrade so valiant, so faithful, so able and so honest as you have always been; but in serving a cause, comradeships have got to be sacrificed. The cause must be held superior to all such considerations. But this dissolution of comradeship—if dissolution must come—in no way affects our personal intimacy. We have long become members of the same family, and we remain such in spite of grave political differences. I have the good fortune to enjoy such relations with several people. To take Sastri for instance, he and I differ in the political outlook as poles as under, but the bond between him and me that sprung up before we knew the political differences has persisted and survived the fiery ordeals it had to go through.

I suggest a dignified way of unfurling your banner. Write to me a letter for publication showing your differences. I will print it in *Young India* and write a brief reply. Your first letter I destroyed after reading and replying to it, the second I am keeping, and if you do not want to take the trouble of writing another letter, I am prepared to publish the letter that is before me. I am not aware of any offensive passage in it. But if I find any, you may depend upon my removing every such passage. I consider that letter to be a frank and honest document.

With love,
Bapu

---

1. In reply to the addressee's letter, dated 11-1-1928; *vide* Appendix "Letter from Jawaharlal Nehru".
2. *Vide* Addenda—2, "Letter to Jawaharlal Nehru", 15-1-1928.
3. *Vide* "The National Congress", 5-1-1928 and "Independence *v.* Swaraj", 12-1-1928.

---

13. Letter to Jawaharlal Nehru

Satyagraha Ashram,
Sabarmati,
February 26, 1928

My Dear Jawahar,

I have your letters. I am sensing all that is going on in Delhi and can understand every word of what you have said in your letter. I can't give you an adequate conception of my grief as I follow the Conference proceedings from day-to-day and read between the lines.

Father's illuminating letter only confirmed my own reading from a distance. Then came Kripalani's letter yesterday to Krishnadas, and yours has come today to put the finishing touch.[1] What a miserable show we are putting up against the insolence of Lord Birkenhead and the crookedness of the Commissioners? I had not expected much from Sir John Simon, but I was not at all prepared for his resorting to all the known tricks of bureaucracy, and this the latest trade on untouchables adds to the ugliness of the whole picture. However, we have to be patient. You must therefore patiently go through the agony and mend where you can.

Do come as early as possible. I hope Kamala is keeping up her strength, if not actually adding to it. I wonder if Father has told you that, before you came, when Father was with me in Bangalore, he and I had contemplated your stay in Bangalore because of its magnificent climate during summer. There are just four weeks of somewhat trying weather, but you could always go to Nandi Hill only 35 miles from Bangalore where you have delightfully cool weather. In no case should Kamala be allowed to lose what she gained in Switzerland.

Yours sincerely,

1. In his letter, dated Allahabad, February 23, Jawaharlal Nehru had written: "I wrote to you a few hours ago and informed you that I hoped to be in Sabarmati on Monday or Tuesday night. Immediately after I received a summons from Delhi to go there and remain there for the next fortnight or more to assist in Constitution drafting.... Personally I have had enough of this All-Parties Conference. After ten days of it, the strain was too great for me and I fled to avoid riot and insurrection! I feel better already after a three-day absence, but another dose of all the parties may go to my head. I am thus not at all desirous of attending the meetings in Delhi. But I do not know what might happen. I shall wire to you from Delhi" (S.N. 13079).

14. Letter to Jawaharlal Nehru

Satyagraha Ashram,
Sabarmati,
March 20, 1928

My Dear Jawahar,

I have received your two letters. I write just now only to fulfil the promise to send you a message for the friend you mentioned.[1] He has now written directly to me, but as I promised the message to you, here it is.

I hope you are following my articles on boycott and mills. I am having conferences with the mill-owners also. Whether they will come to anything I do not know. But if anything appears to you wrong or weak you will please let me know.

How is Kamala doing? Where are you going to keep her during the hot season?

Yours sincerely,

1. *Vide* the following items.

15. Letter to Jawaharlal Nehru

The Ashram,
Sabarmati,
April 5, 1928

My Dear Jawahar,

You will see my article[1] on mills in the current issue of *Young India.* The latest move is on their own to start a Swadeshi League without reference to us. Do not think anything concrete is going to come out of my effort. By all means let them prosecute their own plans. So far as I can see, we must confine our attention to *khadi* hawking.

No final decision has yet been arrived at about the European visit. I am shirking it and making it depend upon some further indication from Rolland which I should have next week.

Yours sincerely,
Bapu

1. *Vide* "A Mill-owner on Boycott", 5-4-1928.

16. Letter to Jawaharlal Nehru

The Ashram,
Sabarmati,
April 8, 1928

My Dear Jawahar,

I have your letter. I do not remember Father having told me that he would be back in Bombay to confer with the mill owners during the last week of this month. But he and I discussed the question of foreign cloth boycott at length and he had a conference with Seth Lalji, Shantikumar, Seths Ambalal, Kasturbhai and Mangaldas. It was a good conference, but nothing definite was done. I have now heard that the mill-owners are going to start their own Swadesh League which means of course that we are not coming to any terms.

The *Ashram*[1] had a long discussion with Lalaji today, for he was here for two days. He is enthusiastic about boycott of foreign cloth. I have supplied him with literature. He even suggested that I should invite a few leaders and confer with [them] about boycott. I told him I had not the courage to do so. He is of opinion that if intense boycott propaganda is to be taken up, I must not go out of the country, wherein of course I agree; but I cannot take up intense propaganda unless politically-minded India is wholeheartedly with me and unless the agitation about temporary boycott of British cloth, principally British cloth, is given up. We have, therefore, come to this provisional arrangement that if anything concrete takes place by spontaneous action on the part of the known leaders, I should give up the idea of going to Europe. On the other hand [if] nothing of that kind happens and if otherwise I see my way clear, I should proceed and that Lalaji and others who are minded like him should cultivate an atmosphere for intense propaganda about foreign cloth boycott with or without the assistance of mills. I therefore suggest that you should confer with Dr. Ansari and others. I suppose they will all go to the Punjab and pass the resolution about foreign cloth boycott through *khadi*. I would warn you against any mention of indigenous mill-cloth. You can simply say: "Whereas the only effective means of immediately demonstrating the united strength of the nation lies through boycott of foreign cloth, this Conference urges all concerned completely to boycott foreign cloth and adopt hand-spun and hand woven *khadi* even though such adoption may necessitate revision of one's taste about dress and some pecuniary sacrifice." You will also let me know the result of private discussions you may have with friends and advise me as to whether I should give up the idea of going to Europe. Dr. Ansari should really be able to decide.

Yours sincerely,

---

17. Letter to Jawaharlal Nehru

The Ashram,
Sabarmati,
April 17, 1928

My Dear Jawahar,

I have your letter. Do you know that even when you wrote to me that you were going to the Punjab, I did not know that you were going as the president of the Conference? When Dr. Kitchlew wrote to me, he said nothing about who the president was to be. However, I was glad when I learnt that you presided.

Of course, I notice everywhere what you noticed at the Conference. I wonder if you have noticed what I sense everywhere, utter absence of seriousness and disinclination to do any concrete work demanding sustained energy.

Do you find any hope in the Punjab for Hindu-Muslim unity?

About the European visit, I can give you no definite news yet.

The fiasco about mills you know everything [of] by this time from Father.

---

18. Letter to Jawaharlal Nehru

The Ashram,
Sabarmati,
April 24, 1928

My Dear Jawahar,

I have your letter. Of course, you know already the calamity that has befallen me on the death of Maganlal. It is well-nigh unbearable.

However, I am putting on a brave front.

I had not read the resolution asking the Congress to drop "peaceful and legitimate means" and change the expression into "by all possible means". Independence I can swallow, "by all means" is unswallowable. But I suppose we shall have to develop stomach strong enough to swallow any poison. I hope however that you will not allow yourself to be exploited beyond your wish and capacity.

The mill-owners, it has now become obviously clear, wanted to do a deal with the Congress. But I am not sorry for these abortive negotiations. They have cleared the atmosphere.

The expected letter from Romain Rolland was received on Sunday. He will not bear the burden I wanted him to do. So, I am not going this year. But you will read about this in the pages of *Young India*.[1]

Yours sincerely,

---

1. *Vide* "To European Friends", 26-4-1928.

19. Letter to Jawaharlal Nehru

July 29, 1928

My Dear Jawaharlal,

I do hope Kamala and Indu are flourishing. I had your wire and letter. The Presidential business is now finished.

I write this to consult you about Bhuvarji. He asks the Ashram to give him Rs. 20 per month and for this he wants Rs. 100 in advance. I would like you to tell me how he is working and whether he is giving you satisfaction. The A.I.S.A. will not and cannot give him anything.

Do you advise the Ashram to supply his needs? What is the nature of work he is doing?

Yours sincerely,
Bapu

---

20. Letter to Jawaharlal Nehru

Satyagraha Ashram,
Wardha,
November 28, 1928

My Dear Jawahar,

I have your letter. I shall be sorry indeed if you have to enter the Municipality again, unless you enter it on condition of perfect obedience being rendered to you. If you have to go in for the purpose of settling disputes, it is not worthwhile. My conviction is that you cannot combine all-India work with solid municipal work. Solid municipal work is a thing complete in itself and requires all the energy that a man can give it and I would not like your work to be anything but solid.

I was to have gone to Mysore to attend the Christian Convention. That was the hope I had given to friends during the middle of the year, but I informed them about a month ago that my going was impossible, if I was to have any rest at all.

The news you had given me about Kamala is bad. I like the idea of her being under treatment in Calcutta. She will have there the best medical advice possible.

I do hope that you will find time to attend the meeting here.

Yours sincerely,
M. K. Gandhi

Pandit Jawaharlal Nehru
Anand Bhawan, Allahabad

---

21. Letter to Jawaharlal Nehru

Ashram,
Sabarmati,
January 12, 1929

My Dear Jawahar,

I have your telegram.[1] I had certainly intended to tour in some parts of the U.P. in response to a request made by some workers in Banda and Jhansi. But they withdrew the request, being diffident. The tour, therefore, was cancelled. There is yet another in prospect and that is near Meerut and Delhi. They want me to go there in March.

But for March I have so many engagements from which I have got to choose. There is Andhra, there is Karnatak and there is Burma besides Delhi and Meerut; and there is also the Punjab. Lalaji's Society people want me there for their anniversary celebration. I am awaiting Father's decision as to the proposed European visit. If he cancels that visit, then the way will be open for me to satisfy all the demands upon my time. If he wants the European visit to come off, then I may not extend my tour beyond the first week of April. I cannot take the matter any further just now. But I would like you to help me to make my choice. You will consult Father about his wishes and that will enable you to guide me better.

By the time this reaches you, Father will have probably telegraphed to me his opinion. If he has not, please see that he does.

How is Kamala doing now? And how are you yourself faring?

You have become Secretary. I want you to throw yourself heart and soul therefore into the programme, and compel obedience to instructions from the Working Committee and try to bring order out of the existing disgraceful disorder.

Yours sincerely,
Bapu

1. Dated January 11, 1929, It read: "Papers announce you touring North United Provinces. Hope you will extend tour South also."

22. Letter to Jawaharlal Nehru

Satyagraha Ashram,
Sabarmati,
January 17, 1929

My Dear Jawarhar,

I have your letter.[1] About the tour in the U.P. I have written to you already.[2] I write this about Kripalani. Jamnalalji tells me that you want Kripalani to take up organization under you, that is to say, to take up the work that Sitla Sahai was doing and add to it as much as he can. Your letter under reply does not quite give me that impression.

Kripalani himself, I understand, has written to you already, because on the strength of Jamnalalji's letter, I had begun to talk to him before receipt of your letter and so had Shankerlal. You will now write to me therefore what you exactly intend in this matter.

If I do not tour in the U.P. in the near future and if you can come over to Sabarmati even for a day or two, we can discuss many things. I utterly distrust doctors' reports about Kamala whether they are favourable or unfavourable. I wish you and Father and Kamala will make up your minds for her to take the natural treatment, that means Kuhne's bath and sun baths. Sun baths are now in vogue even amongst the medical profession and very extraordinary results are claimed for them.

You will telegraph if necessary about Kripalani.

Yours sincerely,
Bapu

1. Dated January 12, 1929 (S.N. 15277).
2. *Vide* "Letter to Jawaharlal Nehru", January 12, 1929.

23. Letter to Jawaharlal Nehru

Satyagraha Ashram,
Sabarmati, B.B.C.I. Rly.,
April 3, 1929

My Dear Jawahar,

I have your letter. As things are, the Andhra people have not left me a single day to enable me to go to the Ashram and then to come to Bombay, and as now the May part of the tour is really for my recreation, I would not like to leave Bombay for Allahabad on the 27th May. But I would like to come to the Ashram for a few days and then go to Almora. I could still do Cawnpore, Allahabad and Lucknow before leaving for Almora, and could even go to the Punjab if the people in the Punjab so require it. No announcement therefore need just now be made, but if you want to fix the date in advance for Cawnpore and Lucknow and even for Almora, let it be a date after 10th of June. I would like to give a clear week to the Ashram before I move out. I would like you to ascertain from the Punjab people what they would have me to do.

I have not got the Andhradesh programme rigidly fixed yet. For the time being therefore you would use Bezwada as headquarters. I expect to reach Bezwada on the 8th instant.

I would like Sitla Sahai to come here if he is not required there for the time being. I want him to be here with reference to his wife and daughter, especially so during my absence.

I send the measurements for Padma's glasses which please hand over to him. I promised to get those measurements and have them sent over to him.

Yours Sincerely,
Bapu

---

24. Letter to Jawaharlal Nehru

April 29, 1929

My Dear Jawahar,

I never get the time to write to you. I have gone through the

Bareilly report. It says nothing, so far as I can see, about the prospect of *khadi*. Have you read it? What do you propose about it?

As for the tour, you would arrange as you think best. Prabhudas wrote an urgent letter. I have told him, I should be ready to go after 10th June and that he should fix the programme in consultation with you.

This tour is somewhat trying but I am taking it very well indeed.

I saw a summary of your speech on the tomb[1]—I liked it.

Yours,
Bapu

[PS.]
My tour programme has been sent to you.

---

1. Slip for 'bomb'?

---

25. Letter to Jawaharlal Nehru

Kavali,
May 10, 1929

My Dear Jawahar,

What a weight upon your mind to have both Kamala and Krishna with the severe attacks you have described. I suppose these domestic troubles must also be taken as part of national discipline. I am glad that Krishna does not require an operation.

You may not know that Andhradesha is noted for nature-cure men and some of them are really brave fellows, brave in the sense that they relentlessly pursue the search without counting the cost. This remedy has in many cases answered where everything else has failed.

And it has the merit of simplicity combined with perfect harmlessness even where it may not result in a cure. I wish you would turn your attention to these cures. Of course in this strict dieting plays a most important part. Where patients do not submit to the dietetic prescriptions, the treatment becomes valueless.

I take it that in spite of Bengal's desire for a postponement, A.I.C.C. will meet on the advertised date.

I had your telegram about Almora. I shall hope to leave Ashram after the tenth of June so as to reach Almora on the 15th.

Yes, you can have me for U.P. and the Punjab and Delhi for the whole of September and October, if October is also wanted. About the Allahabad Municipal Board, you shall decide. I am fed up with addresses. You may therefore accept on my behalf if there is any political or other advantage to be derived from it. If I have received any communication from the Board I have no recollection of it.

Andhra P.C.C. has asked for extension of time up to June on the plea that most of the Congress workers are busy in their own districts with arrangements for the tour and hence are unable to supply the information I wanted. This fact in itself is an evidence of the chaos that reigns supreme in our house. For what I see throughout Andhra is true almost of every province.

I have failed to get any satisfaction from Utkal.

I expect the Tamilnad Secretary on Sunday at Nellore.

I have written[1] to Ghanshyamdas Birla instead of Ramjeebhai to find an auditor of repute for auditing Bengal P. C. C.'s accounts.

Yours sincerely
Bapu

1. *Vide* "Letter to G.D. Birla", 8-5-1929.

---

26. Letter to Jawaharlal Nehru

July 20, 1929

My Dear Jawaharlal,

I have glanced at the programme. So far as I am concerned it is all right. I think I shall easily stand it. I have not checked it for Mondays.

Pyarelal, Devdas and Kusumbehn will be with me. Vallabhbhai, Mahadev and Manibehn will reach *via* Jubbulpore. I do not think there will be any other company with me.

You will please not detain me on 28th. I would like to get away by the first train after finishing on 27th.

I hope Kamala is better. I do want to see her healthy and bright when I come to Allahabad.

Yours,
Bapu

---

27. Letter to Jawaharlal Nehru

On the Train,
July 29, 1929

My Dear Jawaharlal,

Your letters[1] to Indu are excellent and should be published. I wish you could have written them in Hindi. Even as it is there should be a simultaneous publication in Hindi.

Your treatment of the subject is quite orthodox. The origin of man is now a debatable subject. The origin of religion is a still more debatable matter. But these differences do not detract from the value of your letters. They have a value derived not from the truth of your conclusions but from the manner of treatment and from the fact that you have tried to reach Indu's heart and open the eyes of her understanding in the midst of your external activities.

I did not want to strive with Kamala over the watch I have taken away. I could not resist the love behind the gift. But the watch will still be kept as a trust for Indu. In the midst of so many little ruffians about me, I could not keep such a piece of furniture. I would therefore be glad to know that Kamala will reconcile herself to Indu getting back her darling watch.

My article on the Congress crown[2] is already written. It will be out in the next issue of *Young India*.

Yours,
Bapu

1. Letters from a Father to His Daughter.
2. *Vide* "Who Should Wear the Crown", 1-8-1929.

28. Letter to Jawaharlal Nehru

August 22, 1929

My Dear Jawaharlal,

I am delighted over Kamala's operation. I hope she will be fully restored now.

You may depend upon my not unduly pressing your name on

the country. I felt bound to express my opinion to the committee at Lahore in reply to their wire.[1] It is enough for your self-respect that you do not want the crown. It is an ugly business for anybody this time. I have simply pressed your name as of a principle. If the country is not ready to assert that principle, we can wait.

If you are not to be the helmsman, the only alternative I can think of at this juncture is re-election of Father, or failing that, of Dr. Ansari. Can you think of any other name?

I am preparing for the U.P. tour. I am daily recovering lost strength. I am in no way sorry for my experiment from which I have learnt a lot.

Yours,
Bapu

---

1. *Vide* "Telegram to Indian National Congress, Lahore", 19-8-1929.

---

29. Letter to Jawaharlal Nehru

Aligarh,
November 4, 1929

My Dear Jawaharlal,

I have just got your letter. How shall I console you? Hearing others describe your state, I said to myself, "Have I been guilty of putting undue pressure on you?" I have always believed you to be above undue pressure. I have always honoured your resistance. It has always been honourable. Acting under that belief I pressed my suit.

Let this incident be a lesson. Resist me always when my suggestion does not appeal to your head or heart. I shall not love you the less for that resistance.

But why are you dejected? I hope there is no fear of public opinion in you. If you have done nothing wrong, why dejection? The ideal of independence is not in conflict with greater freedom. As an executive of ficer now and President for the coming year, you could not keep yourself away from a collective act of the majority of your colleagues. In my opinion your signature[1] was logical, wise and otherwise correct. I hope therefore that you will get over your dejection and resume your unfailing cheerfulness.

The statement you may certainly make. But there is no hurry about it at all. Here are copies of two cables[2] just received. Please show them to Father too.

If you feel like talking things over with me, do not hesitate to catch me wherever you like.

I hope to see Kamala hale and hearty when I reach Allahabad. If you can do wire that the blues are over.

Yours,
Bapu

1. On the All-Parties Leaders' Joint Statement of November 2, 1929.
2. *Vide* footnote 1, "Cable to *"Daily Express"*, 3-11-1929 and footnote 1 to "Letter to A. Fenner Brockway", 14-11-1929.

30. Telegram to Jawaharlal Nehru

Muttra,
November 6, 1929

Jawaharlal Nehru
Anand Bhavan
Allahabad

Deeply appreciate moral difficulty your second letter.[1] But there should be no hurry arriving at decision. Resignation[2] must not be pressed. If still agitated meet me wherever you like.[3]

Yours,
Bapu

1. *Vide* "Letter from Jawaharlal Nehru", 4-11-1929
2. Of the Secretaryship of the A.I.C.C.
3. *Vide* also "Letter to Jawaharlal Nehru", 8-11-1929.

31. Letter to Jawaharlal Nehru

Brindaban,
November 8, 1929

My Dear Jawahar,

I have your letter.[1] You must have got my wire.[2] You must not resign just now. I have not the time to argue out my point. All I know is that it will affect the national cause. There is no hurry and no principle at stake. About the crown[3], no one else can wear it. It never was to be a crown of roses. Let it be all thorns now. If I could have persuaded myself to wear it, I would have done so at Lucknow.[4] The contingency I had in mind when I would be forced to wear it was not of this type. One of them was your arrest and increased repression.

But let us reserve the whole of this for calm and detached discussion when we meet.

Meanwhile may God give you peace.

Yours,
Bapu

1. *Vide* "Letter to Jawaharlal Nehru", 8-11-1929.
2. *Vide* "Telegram to Jawaharlal Nehru", 6-11-1929.
3. Presidentship of the Congress.
4. At the A.I.C.C. meeting held on 28-9-1929.

32. Letter to Jawaharlal Nehru

November 18, 1929

My Dear Jawahar,

Here is my draft.[1] I want you to consider it carefully and take your full share in the discussion tonight. I do not want you to suppress yourself in any way whatsoever except where *you* feel that self-suppression is better than self-expression on particular occasions.

After all we must each serve according to our lights, not borrowed.

Yours,
Bapu

1. *Vide* the following item.

33. Telegram to Jawaharlal Nehru

Ahmedabad,
January 17, 1930

Jawaharlal Nehru
Allahabad

Reading three O'clock this morning para regarding customs currency. Do not like it. If declaration not sent press paragraph referred should read quote customs and currency have been so manipulated as to heap further burdens on the peasantry. British manufactured goods constitute bulk of our imports.

Customs duties betray clear partiality for British manufactures and revenue from them is used not to lessen burden on the masses but for sustaining highly extravagant administration. Still more arbitrary has been Manipulation of exchange ratio which has resulted in millions being drained away from the country unquote.[1]

Gandhi

1. This was substituted in the final declaration; *vide* "Things to Remember for 26th", 23-1-1930.

34. Letter to Jawaharlal Nehru

February 6, 1930

My Dear Jawaharlal,

I never thought you would miss the importance of the 11 points.[1] However, I do not propose to waste your time by arguing when a day or two after this reaches you you will be on your way to Sabarmati. I expect you here for certain on 12th. I hope to satisfy you that our case has been strengthened not weakened by the 11 points.

Will Kamala accompany you?

Yours,
Bapu

Pandit Jawaharlal Nehru
Anand Bhawan,
Allahabad

1. *Vide* "Clearing the Issue", 30-1-1930.

35. Letter to Jawaharlal Nehru

Ras,
March 19, 1930

My Dear Jawaharlal,

You are in for a whole night's vigil but it is inevitable if you are to return before tomorrow night. The messenger will bring you where I may be. You are reaching me at the most trying stage in the march.

You will have to cross a channel at about 2 a.m. on the shoulders of tried fishermen. I dare not interrupt the march even for the chief servant of the nation.

Love.
Bapu

[PS.]
This is the place where Vallabhbhai was arrested. All the hereditary officials of this village have just gone, leaving their resignations in my hands.
Pundit Jawaharlal Nehru

---

36. Telegram to Jawaharlal Nehru

Gujarat Vidyapith,
Ahmedabad,
August 23, 1931

Pandit Jawaharlal Nehru
Anand Bhawan,
Allahabad

Am proceeding Simla tonight Vallabhbhai accompanying. We both consider your presence and Abdul Ghaffar Khan's necessary. Please start.

Bapu

---

37. Letter to Jawaharlal Nehru

September 7, 1931

My Dear Jawaharlal,

We have just left Port Said. The Big Brother joined us here.

Today is my day of silence. We meet tomorrow for a talk. Here are interesting cuttings from the *Daily Mail* and *Daily Telegraph* some friends from shore brought us. They are meant for your amusement and recreation. You may pass them on to Vallabhbhai after you have done with them.

Devdas has given me your further letters to Indira. I have not yet had the time to look at them. My time has been fully taken up with preparing for *Young India* and *Navajivan,* writing letters and keeping some appointments with sleep thrown in.

I hope the situation in U.P. has improved. I am anxious for news from you. I know you will not hesitate to use the cable when necessary.

Are you keeping touch with A. Ghaffar Khan?

How is Jayaprakash doing?

You will know from *Y.I.*[1] all about affectionate messages from Egypt.

Malaviyaji has been keeping very good health. The sea did not trouble him except for one day. Mirabehn had the largest share of seasickness. Pyarelal and Devdas had a fair share. Mahadev has been quite free. And he has worked the most.

Yours,
Bapu

Encl. 3 cuttings.

---

1. Dated September 24, 1931.

38. Cable to Jawaharlal Nehru[1]

[After October 16, 1931]

Jawaharlal Nehru

Allahabad

Your Cable. You should unhesitatingly take necessary steps meet every situation. Expect nothing here.

Bapu

---

1 This was in answer to a cable dated October 16 from the addressee, which read: "Agrarian situation becoming critical. Coercive processes attachments forcible collection rent continued right through without interval. Many ejected tenants proceeded against for criminal trespass many for fear permanently losing land sold cattle belongings borrowed money paid full demand plus extras. Fresh demand now made for current season inadequate remissions threat that if full payment not made within month remission might be cancelled also no objection considered on behalf tenants till full payment made. Condition of *kisans* deplorable thoroughly exhausted after past six months continuous harassment forcible measures. Apparently, process likely be repeated this season also. Allahabad District Congress Committee resolved under circumstances ask permission start *satyagraha* if necessity arises by advising withholding payment rent application for permission made to Vallabhbhai and Provincial Committee. Representative District Kisan Conference being held next week to decide question. Decision likely have far-reaching consequences but question payment or withholding payment must be decided soon vital urgent problem for kisan no delay."

---

39. Letter to Jawaharlal Nehru

May 2, 1933

My Dear Jawaharlal,

As I was struggling against the coming fast, you were before me as it were in flesh and blood. But it was no use. How I wish I could feel that you had understood the absolute necessity of it. The *Harijan* movement is too big for mere intellectual effort. There is nothing so bad in all the world. And yet I cannot leave religion and therefore Hinduism. My life would be a burden to me, if Hinduism failed me. I love Christianity, Islam and many other faiths through Hinduism.

Take it away and nothing remains for me. But then I cannot tolerate it with untouchability—the high-and-low belief. Fortunately, Hinduism contains a sovereign remedy for the evil. I have applied the remedy. I want you to feel, if you can, that it is well if I survive the fast and well also if the body dissolves in spite of the effort to live. What is it after all—more perishable than a brittle chimney piece. You can preserve the latter intact for ten thousand years, but you may fail to keep the body intact even for a minute. And surely death is not an end to all effort. Rightly faced, it may be but the beginning of a nobler effort.

But I won't convince you by argument, if you did not see the truth intuitively. I know that even if I do not carry your approval with me, I shall retain your precious love during all those days of ordeal.

I had your letter which I had thought I would answer at leisure.

Well, God had willed otherwise. I had talks with Krishna. Of Sarup's work in Kathiawar I think I wrote to you. Kamala has not even sent me her address. There has been no letter from her for many days now. When you see her please give her and Indu my love. Kamala must not worry over the fast. If possible send me a wire.[1]

Love from us all.

Yours,
Bapu

---

1. Dated May 5, the addressee's telegram read: "Your letter. What can I say about matters I do not understand? I feel lost in strange country where you are the only familiar landmark and I try to grope my way in dark but I stumble. Whatever happens my love and thoughts will be with you" (*Gandhi-Nehru Papers,* 1933). For Jawaharlal Nehru's letter of the same date, *vide* Appendix "Letter from Jawaharlal Nehru", 5-5-1933.

40. Letter to Jawaharlal Nehru

August 31, 1933

My Dear Jawaharlal,

So, you are out before your time. I hope you got my wire. I had thought that Mother was going back to Allahabad. I expect full report from you.

Indu has been with me fairly often. She is to come again this evening.

If it is at all possible, we must meet soon. But of course you will be held up there if Mother remains bad. I shall expect a full letter from you. It would be as well to send it by registered post.

I am slowly regaining lost strength. I say nothing about the fast as I expect you now know all about it. More when we meet.

Love.

Bapu

---

41. Letter to Jawaharlal Nehru

'Parnakuti', Poona,
September 14, 1933

My Dear Jawaharlal,

I am glad you have written so fully and frankly.[1] When, on my return from London at the end of 1931, I found you to have been suddenly snatched away from me,[2] I felt the separation keenly. I was, therefore, most anxious to meet you and exchange views.[3]

With much of what you have said in your letter I am in complete agreement. The experience gained after the Karachi Congress has, if possible, strengthened my faith in the main resolution and the economic programme[4] referred to by you. I have no doubt in my mind that our goal can be no less than 'Complete Independence'. I am also in whole-hearted agreement with you when you say that without a material revision of vested interests the condition of the masses can never be improved. I believe, too, though I may not go as far as you do, that before India can become one homogeneous entity, the princes will have to part with much of their power and become popular representatives of the people over whom they are ruling today. I can corroborate from first-hand experience much of what you say about the Round Table Conference. Nor have I the slightest difficulty in agreeing with you that in these days of rapid intercommunication and a growing consciousness of the oneness of all mankind, we must recognize that our nationalism must not be inconsistent with progressive internationalism. India cannot stand in isolation and unaffected by what is going on in other parts of the world. I can, therefore, go the whole length with you and say that "we should range ourselves with the progressive forces of the world". But I know that though there is such an agreement between you and me in the enunciation of ideals, there are temperamental differences between us. Thus, you have emphasized the necessity of a clear statement of the goal, but having once determined it, I have never attached importance to the repetition. The clearest possible definition of the goal and its appreciation would fail to take us there if we do not know and utilize the means of achieving it. I have, therefore, concerned myself principally with the conservation of the means and their progressive use. I know that if we can take care of them, attainment of the goal is assured. I feel too that our progress towards the goal will be in exact proportion to the purity of our means. If we can give an ocular demonstration of our uttermost truthfulness and non-violence, I am convinced that our statement of the national goal cannot long offend the interests which your letter would appear to attack. We know that the princes, the *zamindars*, and those who depend for their existence upon the exploitation of the masses, would cease to fear and distrust us, if we could but ensure the innocence of our methods. We do not seek to coerce any. We seek to convert them. This method may appear to be long, perhaps too long, but I am convinced that it is the shortest.

In the main I agree with your interpretation of Sjt. Aney's instructions and my note[5] upon them. I am quite clear in my mind that had those instructions not been issued, the whole movement of civil resistance would have collapsed through growing internal weakness; for Congressmen were deluding themselves into the belief that there were organizations effectively functioning to which they could look for guidance, when, as a matter of fact, under the organized terrorism which the Ordinance Rule means, organized functioning of Congress Committees had become impossible. A false belief in the functioning of organizations, rendered illegal and largely impotent, was fast producing a demoralization which had to be arrested. There is no such thing as demoralization in civil resistance properly applied. You have said rightly that after all "civil disobedience is essentially an individual affair". I go a step further and say that so long as there is one civil resister offering resistance, the movement cannot die and must succeed in the end. Individual civil resisters do not need the aid of an organization. After all an organization is nothing without the individuals composing it. Sjt. Aney's instructions were, therefore, I hold, an affective answer to the Ordinances and if only men and women belonging to the Congress will appreciate the necessity of those instructions with all their implications, the Ordinances will be rendered nugatory, at least so far as the resisters are concerned. They can form a nucleus around which an army of invincible civil resisters can be built up. Nothing ill Sjt.

Aney's instructions or in my note would warrant the supposition that they preclude organized action by Congressmen in any shape or form.

I would like to warn you against thinking that there is no fundamental difference between individual civil resistance and mass civil resistance. I think that the fundamental difference is implied in your own admission that "it is essentially an individual affair". The chief distinction between mass civil resistance and individual civil resistance is that in the latter everyone is a complete independent unit and his fall does not affect the others; in mass civil resistance the fall of one generally adversely affects the rest. Again, in mass civil resistance leadership is essential, in individual civil resistance every resister is his own leader. Then again, in mass civil resistance, there is a possibility of failure; in individual civil resistance failure is an impossibility. Finally, a State may cope with mass civil resistance; no State has yet been found able to cope with individual civil resistance.

Nor may much be made of my statement that an organization which feels its own strength can at its own risk adopt mass civil resistance. While, as an opinion, it is unexceptionable, I know that at the present moment there is no organization that can shoulder the burden. I do not want to raise false hopes.

Now about the secret methods. I am as firm as ever that they must be tabooed. I am myself unable to make any exceptions.

Secrecy has caused much mischief and if it is not put down with a firm hand, it may ruin the movement. There may be exceptional circumstances that may warrant secret methods. I would forgo that advantage for the sake of the masses whom we want to educate in fearlessness. I will not confuse their minds by leading them to think that under certain circumstances, they may resort to secret methods.

Secrecy is inimical to the growth of the spirit of civil resistance. If Congressmen will realize that all property is liable to be confiscated at any moment, they will learn to be utterly independent of it.

I quite agree with you that it is ludicrous for individuals to send notices to the local authorities of their intention to offer a particular form of civil disobedience. We do not want to make a great movement ridiculous. Therefore, when civil resistance is offered it should be offered seriously and in an effective manner, in so far as this is possible, in furtherance of the Congress programme.

I notice one gap in your letter. You make no mention of the various constructive activities of the Congress. They became an integral part of the Congress programme that was framed after mature deliberations in 1920[6]. With civil resistance as the background we cannot possibly do without the constructive activities such as communal unity, removal of untouchability and universalization of the spinning-wheel and *khaddar*. I am as strong as ever about these. We must recognize that whilst the Congressmen can be counted by hundreds of thousands, civil resisters imprisoned have never amounted to more than one lakh at the outside. I feel that there is something radically wrong if paralysis has overtaken the remaining lakhs. There is nothing to be ashamed of in an open confession by those who for any reason whatsoever are unable to join the civil resisters' ranks.

They are also serving the cause of the country and bringing it nearer to the goal who are engaged in any of the constructive activities I have named and several other kindred activities I can add to the list.

Ordinance or no Ordinance, if individual Congressmen and Congresswomen will learn the art of contributing their share to the work of building of the house of independence and realize their own importance, dark as the horizon seems to us, there is absolutely no cause for despair or disappointment.

Finally, if I can say so without incurring the risk of your accusing me of egotism, I would like to say that I have no sense of defeat in me and the hope in me that this country of ours is fast marching towards its goal is burning as bright as it did in 1920; for I have an undying faith in the efficacy of civil resistance. But as you are aware, after full and prayerful consideration, I have decided not to take the offensive during the unexpired period of the sentence of imprisonment that was pronounced against me on the 4th of August last by the court that met in Yeravada Jail. I need not go into the reasons as I have already issued a separate statement[7] about it. This personal suspension, although it may be misunderstood for a while, will show how and when it may become a duty. And if it is a duty, it cannot possibly injure the cause.

Yours,
Bapu

Jawaharlal Nehru
Poona
Bombay Secret Abstracts, Home Department, Special Branch File No. 800(40) (14), pp. 153-61; also *Mahatma*, Vol. III, pp. 308-11.

---

1. For the addressee's letter dated September 13, 1933, "Letter from Jawaharlal Nehru".
2. The addressee was arrested on December 26, 1931, while on his way to see Gandhiji.
3. Gandhiji and Jawaharlal Nehru met and had long discussions from September 10.
4. "Resolution on Fundamental Rights and Economic Changes", 31-3-1931.
5. "Statement on M.S. Aney's Statement", 26-7-1933.
6. Congress Resolution on Non-Co-operation.
7. "Statement to the Press", 14-9-1933.

---

42. Letter to Jawaharlal Nehru

September 24, 1933

My Dear Jawaharlal,

I had a talk today with Jamnalalji about the proposed match. He seems to know the family well. He is decidedly of opinion that the family, apart from Kasturbhai of course, is not as well off as they would appear to be. He is even of opinion that they may be actually in want. I thought I should pass this news on to you. He too is anxious that I should let you have his opinion. Personally, I remain unaffected by it. But he thinks that Krishna should know it. So, far as I can judge, nothing will affect Krishna's choice unless she has something definite against the young man. And she would be quite right. Kasturbhai is strongly of opinion that Krishna's choice is good.

Love to you all.

Bapu

[PS.]

You may succeed in making persons like me not addressing you as Pandit but I see that the adjective will abide with you.

[PPS.]

What I wanted to suggest was that if this marriage comes off and if Mother agrees, the religious ceremony may be performed at Wardha. I know the difficulty. I am thinking selfishly I know. I have simply thrown out the suggestion. Let us see what happens. I am likely to see Kasturbhai.

---

43. Letter to Jawaharlal Nehru

September 28, 1933

My Dear Jawaharlal,

I have your several letters. I had a long chat with Rafi.[1] He will tell you all about it. I adhere to the opinion that it will do no good to have the A.I.C.C. meeting. But that does not mean that it will deeply hurt me if such a meeting was held. On the contrary if a sufficient number desire it, it is their duty to send a requisition for the meeting.

What I feel is that we may not take the initiative. If you personally feel that it is better to hold the meeting even though there is no requisition, you should hold it. I know that I am not in touch even with the opinion of workers. Therefore, my opinion may safely be discounted by those who have a decided opinion the other way.

The other point I would like to clear apart from the impression that Rafi may give you of my talks is about the workers. Whilst I shall try to do what I can, I am firmly of opinion that every province should support its own workers and that every district or tehsil should support its. Unless we reach that state, ours must remain a house of cards. I think that you should take up the begging bowl in the province and set the pace and the example. My ideal is that every worker should find his maintenance from the area he may serve and feel proud of it. Every labourer is worthy of his hire.

The rest from Rafi.

I hope both Ma and Kamala are better. You will tell me in due course what Dr. Bidhan has to say.

Love.

Bapu

[PS.]
Of the personal letters I need say nothing. I hope you had my two letters[2] written ...[3]

---

1. Rafi Ahmed Kidwai.
2. *Vide* "Letter to Jawaharlal Nehru", 23-9-1933 and 24-9-1933.
3. The source is illegible here.

---

44. Letter to Jawaharlal Nehru

October 7, 1933

My Dear Jawaharlal,

I have your two letters. The first did not call for a reply.

I see that Krishna's marriage comes off on 20th inst. I am glad.

I must not attempt to come to Allahabad. It is much better for me to remain in the *purdah* till the medical men declare me to be quite fit.

Herewith a letter[1] for Krishna.

I see Mother is not yet quite out of the wood. Let us hope she will be fit enough to attend the wedding.

Your article[2] for the D.H. I like very much. I am sending it to Agatha for such use as she can make of it. She is a wounderful worker.

Mira had forgotten all about the note of her prison experiences.

Her draft is now ready. It will be sent to you to be handed to Andrews and such other use that you may wish.

I am thinking out what is possible to do for the workers.

What is this I read about Tandon's differences? Have you seen the paragraph?

Love.

Bapu

---

1. *Vide* the preceding item.
2. This is not available.

---

45. Telegram to Jawaharlal Nehru

Wardha,
October 9, 1933

Jawaharlal Nehru
Anand Bhawan, Allahabad

Thank God. Hope mother will be well enough attend forthcoming wedding in good health.

Bapu

---

46. Letter to Jawaharlal Nehru

Wardha,
October 9, 1933

My Dear Jawaharlal,

I had your wire to which I sent a reply in the afternoon. I do hope Mother will be strong enough to attend to the wedding.

I got today the accompanying from Saraladevi.[1] I have told her Indu[2] is left free to do as she chooses and that she is not likely to entertain any marriage proposal as she is still studying. I have told her too that I am forwarding the letter to you. If Indu was at all prepared to consider a marriage proposal, I do regard Dipak[3] to be a good match.

Hardikar[4] and Kamala Chattopadhyay came in today. Hardikar is suffering from fistula and would need an operation. I shall know more tomorrow. Jamnalalji has gone to Bombay for helping a friend who is in financial trouble. He will be back in four days.

My tour commences on 8th November, all being otherwise well.
I am having fair rest.
Kamala never writes nowadays.
Love.

Bapu

---

1. Saraladevi Chowdhrani.
2. Indira Nehru, addressee's daughter.
3. Son of Saraladevi Chowdharani.
4. N.S. Hardikar, founder and Secretary-General of the Hindustani Seva Dal.

---

47. Letter to Jawaharlal Nehru

October 18, 1933

My Dear Jawaharlal,

Herewith two garlands made out of yarn specially spun by me today for the bride and the bridegroom charged with my blessings.

Will you please put them round their necks on my behalf! I hope they will reach you in time.

I cannot help being sorry that the ceremony has been vetoed by Mrs. Hutheesing. But I suppose in these matters I am a back number.

I understand what you say about Dipak. I would write to Sarala Devi in as gentle a manner as I can.

Love to you all.

Bapu

---

48. Letter to Jawaharlal Nehru

Wardha,
October 23, 1933

My Dear Jawaharlal,

I had two wires one from you and the other from Krishna and Raja. Thank God. Mother's bravery commands my worship. I have pictured her to be a personification of quiet, dignified bravery and sacrifice, ever since I have met her.

One thing I have been forgetting to write to you. If ever you feel that you would like to call a meeting of the A.I.C.C., you must not hesitate to call it. You need not mind my disinclination. I am disinclined, because I feel it will make confusion worse confounded and mean waste of energy, time and money. But I may be quite wrong.

Love to you all.

Blessings from
Bapu

---

49. Letter to Jawaharlal Nehru

Unrevised November 1, 1933

My Dear Jawaharlal,

Your several letters to hand. I see you have handed to the Press the two resignations. They should clear the air a bit.

I do not follow the Hindu Sabha activities. They are vicious. It is most unscrupulous if they are making use of my name in connection with *shuddhi.*[1] If you have any literature please pass it on to me. I think that the nationalist Press so called or real has not welcomed its activities and has been known often to condemn it. I do not know anything about the embargo on M.A.K. Azad's book. As to the *Harijan* activities, the complaint is wholly unjustified. My conscience is absolutely clear. So far as you and I are concerned, we can clear our minds and hands by exchanging letters, if you like. I do not know what aggressive action is possible or desirable beyond an emphatic condemnation of specific acts.

As to Gorakhpur, I do not see what can be done. I am finding it hard to get funds for your workers and the Dal people. I am still talking about both. Baba Raghavdas told me he was trying grain collections for the peasants in distress. He is under promise to send me authentic details of persecution.

Nariman[2] was here yesterday. I have advised him to see you and told him that you were my political chief! What else could I do? I stand thoroughly discredited as a religious maniac and predominantly a social worker. I told him that if I felt convinced that the A.I.C.C. members desired discontinuance of C.D. and a council-entry programme.

I would at once ask you to convene a meeting of A.I.C.C. I do not do so because I believe that the majority will insist on a C.D. programme and I do not want to invite the ordinance sword for it. I have told him too that I would not resist any programme that the A.I.C.C. might want though I could not give my approval to the suspension of C.D. I believe Kelkar's[3] attitude to be honest and consistent.

He frankly dislikes N.C.O. and C.D. He would not join the terrorists or whatever they may be called. Then for a man of political activity, council-entry is the only programme such as it is. Hopeless inactivity is the worst of all and should be discountenanced.

I think I have now covered all the points raised in your letters and even not raised. It is nearing 4 a.m.

Hope Mother's progress continuing. Herewith note[4] for Kamala.

Love.

Bapu

---

1. Literally, 'purificatory rite'. Here reconversion to Hinduism.
2. K.F. Narima.
3. N.C. Kelkar.
4. This is not available.

---

50. Letter to Jawaharlal Nehru

Wardha,
November 11, 1933

My Dear Jawaharlal,

I have just returned from a heavy tour programme and having read your letter telegraphed as follows:[1]

It is impossible to give more than one day and more than three hours. It is difficult enough even to give three hours. The programme is so packed that hardly any time is given for rest. Four hours for rest, bath and dinner, have hitherto dwindled down to two. A programme in which tens of thousands of people are concerned cannot easily be postponed or disturbed. The enclosed copy[2] will give you an idea of the work, and where you find hours of rest, except for Friday afternoon, they have been encroached upon, changing the time from 10 a.m. to 2 p.m. to 12 O'clock to 2 p.m.

I entirely agree with you that the proposed conversation will not clarify matters to any satisfactory extent. If the A.I.C.C. meeting is held, I do not know how I shall be able to attend the sittings. Will it not be better for me to abstain from attending? If it is desirable, I will send my views in writing. The opinion I have expressed in my public letter[3] to you is becoming more and more confirmed.

You must have seen Lahiri's statement about the Hijli Prison. It more than confirms Satisbabu's letter. I have heard from the Governor.[4]

His Secretary says that "His Excellency will look into the matter to which you refer."

I have read the appeal for the Hospital.[5] I hope it will have the response it deserves.

I carefully read your letter about the Government demand. In anything you do about Swaraj Bhawan, do you not think that you should consult the trustees and not merely inform them? I have not been able even to show your letter to Jamnalalji for sheer want of time. He twits me by saying that as I am in Wardha you are ignoring him entirely, not even acknowledging his letters. I told him that your letters to me are as much for him as for me and that just now the few of us who are out have little time for performing acts of mere courtesy.

You cannot expect rapid progress for an old patient like Mother. The wonder to me is that she has survived the attack she had.

I hope the progress though slow continues.

Love.

BAPU

Encl.

---

1. *Vide* the preceeding item.
2. *Vide* Appendix "Tour Programme", 7-11-1933.
3. *Vide* "Letter to Jawaharlal Nehru", 14-9-1933.
4. Gandhiji wrote to the Governor of Bengal on November 2, 1933; *vide* "Letter to Governor of Bengal", 1-11-1933.
5. *Vide* "Letter to Jawaharlal Nehru", 30-10-1933.

51. Letter to Jawaharlal Nehru

November 27, 1933

My Dear Jawaharlal,

Here is Gasavi's letter. I am telling him, I see no objection to the Party so long as it is not claimed as the Congress Party and that in any case he should seek your advice.

I note that we are to meet at Jubbulpore on 5th December. I shall try to give more time, if it is at all possible.

Have I not sent you the programme for C.P.? More than that was not ready till now.

So, you are being gradually disburdened of shares and the like. I am not sorry. From my point of view the ideal thing would be a voluntary surrender of all the property you have, either to an institution or to those members of the family who do not want to throw themselves into the battle which is bound to be prolonged and perhaps increasingly bitter. In the final heat only those will be able to stand who have no property and nowhere to rest their heads on. But it is no use worrying over the future. Whatever happens you will be found in the front rank.

I am glad that Mother is making steady progress. I wonder if she knows all that is happening.

Yes, I did read your attack on the Hindu Sabha. It might have been less fierce. The summary made you speak like a partisan.

Love.

Bapu

[P.S.]

You will find the dates in the enclosed programme.

---

52. Letter to Jawaharlal Nehru

December 26, 1933

My Dear Jawaharlal,

Here is a cutting from the *M. Mail.*[1] Though the whole conversation practically referred to you and your views, naturally the interviewer could not reproduce it all. I was shown the proof. It is a fair presentation of the substance of what I said. Please read it carefully and correct me where you find me to have erred about yourself.

There is a great deal of misunderstading about you in our circles too. But it does not worry me.

You will find also the programme[2] so far as it goes.

I hope Mother is progressing.

Love.

Bapu

---

1. *vide* "Interview to Madras Mail".

---

53. Letter to Jawaharlal Nehru[1]

Gauhati,
April 14, 1934

My Dear Jawaharlal,

I got up this morning at 12.15 in order to overtake arrears.

You have been ever in my mind. I hope you will be permitted to receive this letter. I would like a line from you to tell me how you are keeping and what you are doing.

You must have seen my two decisions. That they are almost simultaneous is a mere coincidence. The revival of the Swarajya Party is a right step. There is no doubt that we have in the Congress a body of men who believe in Council-entry and who will do nothing else if they cannot have that programme. Their ambition must be satisfied.

The other decision about confining C.R. to myself so far as the goal is concerned is much the most important. It was inevitable. Having arrived at it, I can see the rightness of the decision for a thousand reasons. I have given the precipitating cause. But the decision was slowly coming to me. I do hope that you have not been upset by it.

You were before my mind's eye the whole time the decision was taking shape. I concluded that, though it might produce a momentary shock, you would ultimately see the truth of it and be glad. I wonder!

We all often talk about you. We are a large party. I was with Mother and the members of the family for nearly two hours when I passed through Allahabad.

Love.

Bapu

---

1. He was in Alipore Central Jail at this time.

54. Letter to Jawaharlal Nehru[1]

August 14, 1934

My Dear Jawaharlal,

Though you are now under distressing circumstances, your release[2] takes a great load off my mind, as it is three-fourths medicine for Kamala. I have missed you greatly during all the momentous steps I have taken. But of these when we meet. I am well, though the last day proved the most trying of all the days and washed me out thoroughly. But I have no doubt that I shall pick up quickly.

This is however to suggest to you that you should not make any public political pronouncement. I have felt that in cases of domestic illness or sorrow the Government has acted in a becoming manner. I do feel therefore that we ought to recognize this fact by not using the liberty thus obtained for any other purpose not inconsistent with that of the Government. I feel that this is due to them and to ourselves, especially when civil resistance is suspended. If my argument appeals to your reason, you will announce your self-restraint in a fitting manner. When Kamala is better I expect you to come here. I shall be in Wardha up to the end of the month, except that I might have to go to Bombay to attend the delicate operation that Jamnalalji might have to go through during the month.

I hope Mama is doing well and so Krishna. You will let me know how you have fared this time in jail.

Love.

Bapu

---

1. An identical telegram (C.W. 7968) was sent G.D. Birla, Biirla Mills, Delhi on the same day.
2. The addressee had telegraphically informed Gandhiji : "I have been permitted to stay with Kamala. The position is not clear. Hope you are well."

---

55. Letter to Jawaharlal Nehru

November 22, 1934

My Dear Jawaharlal,

I sent you a letter some days ago simply inquiring about your health. Mummy who came in yesterday tells me you do not get letters except what is sent in Kamala's packet. I should like to know the rules regulating your correspondence. Please let me know how you are doing and how you are passing your time.

Love.

Bapu

---

56. Letter to Jawaharlal Nehru

Wardha,
September 12, 1935

My Dear Jawaharlal,

How well you have joined Kamala! It is the best tonic for her. I shall keep a note for her herewith. Your messages are being duly received here. And Sarup repeats what she receives. Let us hope all will end well. Please thank Dr. Atal for his messages and letters which have been most helpful. I expect a regular mail from you whilst the crisis lasts. Typed sheets[1] are with me. I shall go through them as soon as possible.

Mahadev had to go to Bombay to help Vallabhbhai about an inquiry. And he is still there. Rajagopalachari has just dropped in with Laxmi and her baby boy. Devdas was badly ill. Ansari has packed him off to Simla. I have Mira on my hands prostrate with bad fever.

I would like you to allow yourself to be elected President for the next year. Your acceptance will solve many difficulties. If you think fit, send me a wire.

Has Indu been fixed up?

Khurshed is here. She will be writing to you by the ordinary mail.

Love from us all.

Bapu

---

1. Of the addressee's autobiography published in 1936.

---

57. Letter to Jawaharlal Nehru

October 3, 1935

My Dear Jawaharlal[1],

Your letters come in with clock-like regularity and they are such a blessing. I see that Kamala is putting forth a very brave effort. It will be rewarded. You know my partiality for nature-cure methods. There are in Germany itself many nature-cure establishments. Kamala's case may be past that stage. But one never knows. I know of cases which were reported to be for surgical treatment but which yielded to nature cure treatment. I send you this experience of mine for what it is worth.

Your letter about the wearing of the next year's crown was delightful. I was glad to have your consent. I am sure that it would solve many difficulties and it is the rightest thing that could have happened for the country. Your presidentship at Lahore[2] was totally different from what it would be at Lucknow[3]. In my opinion it was comparatively plain sailing at Lahore in every respect. It won't be so in any respect at Lucknow. But those circumstances I cannot imagine anybody better able to cope with than you. May God give you all the strength to shoulder the burden.

I am going through your chapters[4] as speedily as I can. They are to me of absorbing interest. More than that I must not say just now.

This letter carries the love of us to you all.

Bapu

Pandit Jawaharlal Nehru

---

1. The addressee was in Germany with his wife Kamala who was undergoing treatment in a sanatorium.
2. In 1929.
3. The Congress session was scheduled to be held in April 1936.
4. Of autobiography.

58. Letter to Jawaharlal Nehru

Wardha,
[October 10, 1935][1]

My Dear Jawaharlal,

I wanted to write to you on Sunday but I was so busy that I simply could not do it. That was to be in answer to your letter enclosing copy of your letter to Agatha.[2] Yours to Agatha gave me an insight into the working of your mind which I would not miss for anything. She fully deserved that frankness. I can endorse most of your sentiments. You do not know that I have written to her more than once in much the same strain though in my own way and my own language. Nevertheless if Kamala shows distinct signs of improvement and if you are free to go [to] London and the way is open, I would like you to see the big ones, open yourself out to them even as you have to Agatha.

But your letter received yesterday shows that you may not leave Kamala's bedside just yet. After all you have been freed for that purpose and if Providence keeps you chained to Kamala's bed, we must not grumble. You have gone there to see her through the terrible ordeal. How I wish I was there to share your burden and cheer Kamala! As I saw her for two days in Bombay before her departure, I observed that she never had so much peace of mind as she seemed to enjoy then. Her faith in the benevolence of God, she said, was never so bright as then. Her mental disturbance had vanished and she did not mind what happened to her. She went to Europe because you all wished it; it seemed to be her obvious duty to do so. If she lives, she will live for greater service than she has yet rendered. If she dies, she will do so to come down to earth with a body more fitted for her task than the one she has today.

It is well too that Indu's[3] literary studies remain suspended for a while. For me, she is having a training that is of far greater value than any she would have in a college. She is having her training in the University of Nature. She may give the finishing touch by completing her literary studies.

I am going through your chapters with the deepest interest. I should like to finish them at a single sitting as Mahadev did and as Khurshed[4] almost did. I have no such good luck. I must reserve my opinion till I have reached the last chapter.[5] I am thankful that you have sent them to me.

I am not going to talk to you about the politics. It is enough for my purpose that you will shoulder the burden, if it falls to your lot.

That it will, seems to me to be a foregone conclusion.

You will read the accompanying to Kamala, if you think fit.

Indu used to write to me a few lines when you were not there. Now I suppose she thinks she is absolved from the task !

Love.

Bapu

[PS.]

You must excuse my obstinacy in writing with village ink, village reed on village paper.

---

1. A part of this letter is available in Mahadev Desai's Diary under this date. The original, which is damaged here, however bears the date 18-10-1935.
2. Agatha Harrison.
3. Indira, addressee's daughter.
4. Dadabhoy Naoroji's grand daughter.
5. *Vide* "Letter to Jawaharlal Nehru", 19-12-1935.

---

59. Letter to Jawaharlal Nehru

Wardha,
October 17, 1935

My Dear Jawaharlal,

Your very important letter to hand. I have wired[1] to Rajendra Babu about Swaraj Bhawan. I do not know what is happening. I am entirely of your opinion that the policy of the Committee should be strictly defined.

As to our attitude on the present world situation, I do not think there is want of appreciation of it. But it is our helplessness which imposes silence on us. There is no weakness either. It is merely a matter, if you will, of tactics in the best sense of the term. Anyway I have no sense in me of weakness. But I know that I cannot speak with effect at this juncture. I cannot give the lead without knowing what the people can do. I know what they should do. And what is true of me is perhaps equally true of the majority of our workers. But I have great faith in you in these matters. You have undoubtedly a much greater grasp of the situation than anyone of us has, certainly than I can ever hope to have. Therefore, you may be able to evolve a dignified formula for national self-expression in speech as well as in action assuming of course that at the present moment direct action is ruled out.

Your paragraph about Kamala is somewhat disturbing. But we are prepared for these ups and downs. I must await your further contribution on the Constitution[2] before I say anything. I am glad I spent the money[3] for putting you in possession of the Constitution as early as it was possible.

Love to you all.

Blessings from
Bapu

---

1. *Vide* the preceding item.
2. Congress constitution.
3. The constitution was sent by air mail and the addressee had protested against this expenditure.

---

60. Letter to Jawaharlal Nehru

April 21, 1936

My Dear Jawaharlal,

The notes make good reading. Your answers were fairly full and of course straight.

Why do you feel worried over the forthcoming meeting[1]? If there is discussion it would only be to convince one another of the soundness of one's views. You will stop the discussion when you think a proposition has been thoroughly argued. After all you want teamwork and I have great hope of this happening.

I reach Nagpur 23rd evening.

I wish Ranjit[2] will take care of himself. I am glad he has gone to Khali. I expect Sarup to accompany you.

Sardar is still suffering and is just now on buttermilk only. I am taking him to Nandi Hill after 8th May. I wish you too could come.

Love.

Bapu

---

1. Of the Congress Working Committee.
2. Ranjit Pandit, addressee's sister's husband.

---

61. Letter to Jawaharlal Nehru

Wardha,
May 3, 1936

My Dear Jawaharlal,

My right hand needs rest. You will perhaps like to read the enclosed.[1] It need not be returned.

Khurshed has written to me about her new suggestion regarding the scope of Kamala Memorial. If it is a substitute for the hospital, it is in my opinion inadmissible. And it cannot be carried out for 3 lacs.

Love.

Bapu

---

1. Presumably a copy of the letter to Agatha Harrison, dated April 30, 1936; Vide also "Letter to Jawaharlal Nehru", 12-5-1936.

---

62. Letter to Jawaharlal Nehru

Unrevised by me Segaon,
July 15, 1936

Dear Jawaharlal,

(1) I hope you got my wire about *The Times of India* letter. I procured it yesterday and read it through. Nobody has ever written to me about the subject-matter. My reading of the letter confirms my view that you should take legal notice of the libel.

(2) If you will not misunderstand me, I would like you to keep me free of the Civil Liberties Union. I do not like for the time being

to join any political institution. And there is no meaning in a confirmed civil resister joining it. Apart however from my joining or not joining the Union, maturer consideration confirms me in my opinion that it would be a mistake to appoint Sarojini Naidu or for that matter any civil resister as President. I am still of opinion that the President should be a well-known Constitutional lawyer. If that does not commend itself to you then, you should have an author of note who is not a law-breaker. I would also ask you to restrict the number of members. You need quality, not quantity.

(3) Your letter is touching. You feel to be the most injured party. The fact is that your colleagues have lacked your courage and frankness. The result has been disastrous. I have always pleaded with them to speak out to you freely and fearlessly. But having lacked the courage, whenever they have spoken they have done it clumsily and you have felt irritated. I tell you they have dreaded you, because of your irritability and impatience of them. They have chafed under your rebukes and magisterial manner and above all your arrogation of what has appeared to them your infallibility and superior knowledge. They feel that you have treated them with scant courtesy and never defended them from socialists' ridicule and even misrepresentation.

You complain of their having called your activities harmful.

That was not to say that you were harmful. Their letter was no occasion for recounting your virtues or your services. They were fully conscious of your dynamism and your hold over the masses and the youth of the country. They know that you cannot be dispensed with.

And so they wanted to give way.

I look upon the whole affair as a tragi-comedy. I would therefore like you to look at the whole thing in a lighter vein. I do not mind your taking the A.I.C.C. into your confidence. But I do want you not to impose on it the unbearable task of adjusting your family quarrels or choosing between them and you. Whatever you do you must face them with accomplished things.

Why do you resent their majority being reflected in all subcommittees etc.? Is it not the most natural thing? You are in office by their unanimous choice but you are not in power yet. To put you in office was an attempt to find you in power, quicker than you would otherwise have been. Anyway that was at the back of my mind when I suggested your name for the crown of thorns.

Keep it on though the head be bruised. Resume your humour at the committee meetings.

That is your most usual role, not that of a care-worn irritable man ready to burst on the slightest occasion.

How I wish you could telegraph to me that on finishing my letter you felt as merry as you were on that New Year's Day in Lahore when you were reported to have danced round the tricolour flag.

You must give your throat a chance.

I am revising my statement. I have decided not to publish it till you have seen it.

I have decided that nobody should see our correspondence, besides Mahadev.

Love.

Bapu

---

63. Letter to Jawaharlal Nehru

Segaon, Wardha,
August 10, 1936[1]

My Dear Jawaharlal,

Khan Saheb has received the usual notice to attend the meetings[2] in Bombay. He has no desire to attend them and I do not want to press him. And in Bombay he will be asked to attend meetings and functions at which he would be called upon to speak. I do not want him to do so just now. I want him rather to pass the year with me. And he is none too strong nor invulnerable to attacks of illness. Will you, therefore, please excuse him from attendance?

Love.

Bapu

1. In this source this letter is placed among 1934 papers and same year in assign to it in A Bunch of old letters. This however is a mistake Gandhiji shifted to Segaon only in 1936.
2. Of the A.I.C.C.

64. Letter to Jawaharlal Nehru

Segaon,
August 28, 1936

My Dear Jawaharlal,

Our conversation of yesterday has set me thinking. Why is it that with all the will in the world I cannot understand what is so obvious to you? I am not, so far as I know, suffering from intellectual decay.

Should you not then set your heart on at least making me understand what you are after? I may not agree with you. But I should be in a position to say so. Yesterday's talk throws no light on what you are after. And probably what is true of me is true of some others. I am just now discussing the thing with Raja. I should like you to discuss your programme with him if you can spare the time. I must not write at length, having no time. You know what I mean.

Love.

Bapu

---

65. Letter to Jawaharlal Nehru

December 28, 1936

My Dear Jawaharlal,

If you finish today, as I hope you will, you will perhaps let me go away tomorrow after midday.

If you have appreciated my suggestion about holding the Congress in villages hereafter, I would like you to ask the Congress to revert to the old rule of holding it in between February and March.

The sufferings of the thousands in wintry weather should be avoided if possible. Parliamentarians should fit in with this arrangement. There is no reason why, if the Congress secures a majority in the legislatures, they should not have vacation as they have during Xmas, Easter etc. I have told Sarup[1] that land somewhere must be secured soon and then house-to-house collections started for Kamala memorial.

Love.

Bapu

---

1. Vijayalakshmi Pandit.

---

66. Letter to Jawaharlal Nehru

January 3, 1937

My Dear Jawaharlal,

I wish I could have gone with you to Ajanta. Before I received your letter, I had spoken strongly to Khan Saheb[1] and urged him to send Mehrtaj[2] to Vakil's school. But he was adamant. He does not want her to go to a mixed school. I spoke to Mehrtaj too. She is undoubtedly restless. But Khan Saheb is sanguine and believes that Mehrtaj will recover her usual cheerfulness.

I do hope you will take care of yourself and not wear yourself out. I had a brief talk with Sarup over the memorial[3]. I am sure that before anything else, at least the ground must be acquired. There need be no insistence on having the plot you described to me or another near Anand Bhawan.

Love.

Bapu

---

1. Extracted from the addressee's article "You Must Not Grieve". The letter, he says, was in response to a sort of "last appeal" against attacks on him from the Government of India, the Congress and the Press.
2. The addressee was the Director-General of the All India Radio.
3. Kamala Nehru Memorial.

67. Telegram to Jawaharlal Nehru

Wardhaganj,
June 14, 1937

Jawaharlal
Care Doctor Bidhan Roy
Wellington Street
Calcutta

I hope you Indu well. Come with her and Maulana during last week weather cooling.

Love.

Bapu

---

68. Letter to Jawaharlal Nehru

Segaon, Wardha,
June 22, 1937

My Dear Jawaharlal,

You letter has just reached me. Though three days might prove too few, they would be better than nothing. It is a pity Indu can't come with you. I had thought that the operation that she had for tonsils many years ago was the last. I take it this would be as simple as the previous one.

Love to you all.

Bapu

---

69. Letter to Jawaharlal Nehru

June 25, 1937

My Dear Jawaharlal,

Just received your statement on the Frontier policy. Khan Saheb and I have read it. I like it very well. I wonder if the Spanish bombing and the British are exactly alike. How has the extent of the British damage been known? What has been the ostensible reason given for the British bombing? Don't smile or be angry that I do not know these things so well as you do. I can learn very little from the little I see of the newspapers. But don't trouble to answer my questions. I shall follow the reactions to your statement. Maybe these will throw some light. And in any case you will fill in the gaps when we meet. I hope the Maulana will come. But even if he cannot I would like you to hold on to the date. Let us have the three quiet days.

Hope Indu is well.

Love.

Bapu

[PS.]
Khan Saheb wants you to see the enclosed.

---

70. Letter to Jawaharlal Nehru

July 10, 1937

My Dear Jawaharlal,

I had long chats with Maulana Saheb yesterday. If he is to be consulted in the choice of Muslim Ministers in the Provinces, I think it is better to make the public announcement to the effect. The Maulana agrees. If you think that the Working Committee should be consulted, I would suggest consultation by wire.

I expect you will write on the Hindi-Urdu topic at an early date.[1]

Yours sincerely,
Bapu

---

1. Jawaharlal Nehru write an essay entitled "The Question of Languages" for the Congress Political and Economic Studies Series. For extracts from it and Gandhiji's Foreward, dated August 3, 1937.

71. Letter to Jawaharlal Nehru

Segaon, Wardha,
July 15, 1937

Unrevised

My Dear Jawaharlal,

Today is the election day. I am watching.

But this I write to tell you that I have begun to write on the function of Congress Ministries and allied topics.[1] I hesitated but I saw that it was my duty to write, when I felt so keenly. I wish I could send you an advance copy of my article for *Harijan*. Mahadev will see this. If he has a copy he will send it. When you see it, you will please tell me if I may continue to write so. I do not want to interfere with your handling of the whole situation. For, I want the maximum from you for the country. I would be doing distinct harm, if my writing disturbed you.

I hope you got my letter[2] about the Maulana.

Love.

Bapu

---

1. *Vide* "Congress Ministries", 17-7-1937; also "The Fundamental Difference", 24-7-1937.
2. *Vide* "I Letter to Amrit Kaur", 10-7-1937.

---

72. Letter to Jawaharlal Nehru

Segaon, Wardha,
July 22, 1937

My Dear Jawaharlal,

Maulana Saheb stopped for a day in Wardha and we had a long chat. He showed me the draft agreement between Muslim League members of the Assembly and the Congress members.[1] I thought it was a good document. But he told me that whilst you liked it, Tandonji did not. I have written to the latter about it as the Maulana suggested I should. What is the objection?

The Rs. 500 salary with big house and car allowances is being severely criticized.[2] The more I think of it, the more I dislike this extravagant beginning. I talked about this, too, to the Maulana.

How is Indu?

Love.

Bapu

---

1. *Vide* also letter to the addressee, "Letter to Jawaharlal Nehru", 10-7-1937.
2. *Vide* also "Letter to Vallabhbhai Patel", 19-7-1937.

---

73. Letter to Jawaharlal Nehru

Segaon, Wardha,
July 30, 1937

My Dear Jawaharlal,

I hope Mahadev told you yesterday in addition to acknowledging your essay on Hindi[1] that the Viceroy had invited me to Delhi on the 4th for no special reason but merely to have the pleasure of meeting him. I replied[2] saying that he had anticipated me for I wanted to seek an interview with him about the ban on Khan Saheb and my desire to visit the Frontier. I am accordingly reaching Delhi on the 4th. The appointment is for 11.30. Therefore, I hope to be able to leave the same day, returning to Segaon on the 5th.

But this letter is to send you a copy of Zakir's letter in reply to my letter giving my reaction to the recent riot in Bombay and the wretched Hindi-Urdu controversy. I thought that I should share with you this considered letter.

I do not regard the Jhansi election as a rout. It is an honourable defeat, giving rise to the hope that if we plod away we can effectively take the Congress message to the Mussalmans. But I still abide by my opinion that the mere taking of the message unaccompanied by substantial work in the villages won't answer our purpose in the end.

But it all depends upon the way in which we want to generate power.

Meherally's speech in Madras is an eye-opener for me. I wonder how far he represents the general socialistic view. Rajaji has sent me a cutting containing his speech. I hope he has sent a copy to you also. I call it a bad speech of which you should take notice. This is going contrary to the Congress policy as I read it.

There is also Roy's speech at Madras. I take it, you get all such cuttings. Nevertheless, for ready reference I enclose the cuttings which Pyarelal has made for me. Roy has been writing to me, too. You should see his latest letter. It will go with this if I have not destroyed it.

What is your reaction to his attitude? As I have already told you I find it difficult to understand him.[3]

Your calling *khadi* 'livery of freedom'[4] will live as long as we speak the English language in India. It needs a first-class poet to translate into Hindi the whole of the thought behind that enchanting phrase. For me it is not merely poetry but it enunciates a great truth whose full significance we have yet to grasp.

Love.

Bapu

[PS.]

Though the paragraph about Roy's speech follows the one about Meherally's it is not to suggest that it is on a par with M's.

1. *Vide* footnote 1, "Letter to Mirabehn", 10-7-1937.
2. *Vide* "Letter to Lord Linlithgow", 27-7-1937.
3. *Vide* also "Letter to M.N. Roy", 27-7-1937.
4. Jawaharlal Nehru used this phrase in his appeal to the country to celebrate August 1 as 'Ministry Day'; *vide* "Livery of Freedom", 31-7-1937.

74. Letter to Jawaharlal Nehru

On the Train,
August 4, 1937

My Dear Jawaharlal,

I am stupid. On receiving your letter I searched my file and behold! I found the cutting containing Meherally's speech. I referred to his, not Masani's speech.[1]

This is being written in a terribly jolting train taking me back to Wardha. It is now 10.30 p.m. I woke up from sleep, thought of the speech and began the search. Yesterday's compartment was better.

I saw the Viceroy. You will have seen the communique.[2] It correctly summarizes the interview. There were other incidental things which Kripalani will mention to you when he meets you. One thing I may mention here. He might invite you as he invited me. I told him that if the invitation was sent, you were not likely to refuse it. Was I right?

I am sorry for having inflicted Roy's speeches on you.[3] But I think you were bound to read them. However, I am in no hurry to have your opinion on them. You may take your time unless you have already read them. I note that you are having the operation for Indu in Bombay.

Love.

Bapu

---

1. *Vide* "Letter to Jawaharlal Nehru", 30-7-1937.
2. Issued after the interview on August 4, it read: "...The Viceroy listened with interest to Mr. Gandhi's views on the matters in question and undertook to intimate them to the Governor of the North-West Frontier Province. The interview was entirely general and personal in character, the principal subject of discussion being rural uplift and improvement of the conditions of the peasantry."
3. *Vide* "Letter to Jawaharlal Nehru", 30-7-1937.

---

75. Letter to Jawaharlal Nehru

Segaon, Wardha,
August 8, 1937

My Dear Jawaharlal,

I forgot to cover one point in your letter referring to Meherally's speech. I mean Rajaji's communique releasing the summer school prisoners. I had read it before receiving your letter. But it did not offend me. I suppose because you approved of the action of the students of the summer school and I could not defend it anyway whatsoever.[1] I think that it was necessary to draw attention to the fact that the release did not mean approval of this breach or the offence which in law it was. I fear that often when the Congress is in power it will use language which its predecessors have used and yet the motive behind will be different.

I hope you will have a nice time in Bombay over the operation. You will wire when it is over.

Love.

Bapu

[PS.]

If Nariman comes to you please grant him the permission to have the inquiry. I am sorry you will be bothered about this affair in Bombay. Mahadev will tell you what I have been doing.

Bapu

---

1. For Jawaharlal Nehru's statement on Kottapatam Summer School, *vide* "The Kottapatam Summer School".

---

76. Letter to Jawaharlal Nehru

October 12, 1937

My Dear Jawaharlal,

I have your letter. I am trying to come to Calcutta, leaving here on the 25th. You will then tell me all about the ministerial deeds in the Congress Provinces. I do hope that the sore throat and cold were only temporary things, and that you were able to stand the strain in the Punjab. The climate in the Frontier must be very delightful. How I wish you would take things easy for a time at least!

Love.

Bapu

---

77. Letter to Jawaharlal Nehru

1 Woodburn Park,
Calcutta
November 1, 1937

My Dear Jawaharlal,

Enclosed herewith is the judgement of the inquiry committee about the two issues raised by Shri Nariman in his correspondence with you and me.[1] I had thought that Shri Nariman's acceptance of my recommendation to make a confession[2] which was to take the place of the judgement was a fair ending to an inquiry which gave me many an anxious moment. But Shri Nariman's recantation of the confession which I first saw only in the Press alters the position and reveals the painful state of Shri Nariman's mind. The recantation contains a patent untruth as pointed out by me in my letter[3] to Shri Nariman which you will find in the enclosure.

I recall the fact that Shri Nariman himself courted the inquiry and deliberately wanted an investigation into the charge made on him by Sardar Vallabhbhai of a grave breach of trust in the matter of the Bombay election in 1934. In his letter addressed to you occurs the following sentence:

If the verdict of such an independent tribunal and enquiry tends to blame me in the slightest degree, then I will willingly submit to any penalty which you or any other authority chooses to impose, but at the same time hoping and expecting that, if the blame is found elsewhere, similar indiscriminating judgement should follow regardless of personalities or personal considerations.

In his letters to me (I have not the copies with me), he went further and said that, if he was found guilty of the Sardar's charge, he would consider himself to be unworthy of holding any office of trust.

I am of opinion that by his conduct Shri Nariman has proved himself unworthy of holding any position of trust, not only because he has been found guilty of grave breach of trust in 1934 election and has failed to prove the charge brought by him against Sardar Vallabhbhai, but by his subsequent conduct as betrayed in the correspondence, and especially by his unfortunate recantation of the confession freely given by him in the presence of his counsel.

Yours sincerely,
M. K. Gandhi

Shri Jawaharlal Nehru
President, A.I.C.C.

---

1. *Vide* "Note on Nariman-Sardar Case", 14-10-1937.
2. *Vide* "Statement to the Press", 16-10-1937, and "K.F. Nariman's Statement".
3. Dated October 29, 1937; *vide* "Letter to K.F. Nariman", 29-10-1937.

78. Letter to Jawaharlal Nehru

On Way to Wardha,
November 18, 1937

My Dear Jawaharlal,

I fancy I could read the personal letter in your eyes as you were hovering round me that awful Sunday night and silent Monday. The weakness has not yet left me. I need prolonged rest from all mental toil, but that perhaps cannot be had.

This I write to report to you what I have done about the prisoners in Bengal, and to ascertain whether it meets with your approval.

The negotiations have been a taxing affair. Before entering upon them I had consulted the two Brothers[1] as to the desirability of securing relief through negotiations. It was possible to be indifferent as to the result and rely upon the growth of public opinion forcing release whenever it was to come. The Brothers were emphatically for negotiations, whilst public agitation continued. I unfolded my plan also and it was after the style of my telegram[2] to the Andamans prisoners. And so I saw the repatriates[3], detenus brought back from Deoli and last night the Hijli prisoners. The Ministers have agreed to release what they call 'village and home domiciled' detenus almost forthwith, and inside of four months to release those in the detenu camps whom they may consider to be safe. For the rest they will accept my recommendation, if they are not earlier released. My recommendation will depend upon my ascertaining the present belief of the detenus. If I am able to say to the Government that they do not believe in methods of violence for the attainment of independence and that they will pursue such Congress activities as are approved of by the Congress from time to time, they will release them. A declaration of policy might be made any time. I need not go into the details of the conversations with the prisoners in the several prisons and in Hijli camp. I wonder if all this commends itself to you. If you strongly disapprove of it, I would like you to telegraph. Otherwise I shall await your letter.

The strikes in Ahmedabad of which I have no knowledge, except from what I gather from the papers, as also what the papers say about Sholapur,[4] disturbed me. If we cannot control the situation either because a section of the Congressmen would not submit to

Congress discipline or because the Congress cannot control the activities of those who are outside the Congress influence, our holding of offices is bound to prove detrimental to the Congress cause.

The '*Bande Mataram*' controversy has not yet died out. Many Bengalis are sore at heart over the W.C. decision.[5] Subhas told me he was trying to calm the atmosphere.

I expect to have to go back to Bengal soon after the assumption of office by the incoming Governor.

I hope you are keeping well. The paragraph in the newspaper about Sarup[6] was disturbing. Is her health unequal to the strain she is undergoing?

This is being written as we are nearing Nagpur. We arrive Wardha this evening.

Love,

Bapu

---

1. Subhas Chandra Bose and Sarat Chandra Bose.
2. *Vide* "Telegram to Viceroy", 27-8-1937 and "Letter to Mahadev Desai", 3-9-1937.
3. On October 30.
4. *Vide* "Storm Signals."
5. Some Muslims having objected to the practice of singing *Bande Mataram* in certain legislatures, the Working Committee recommended that "whenever and wherever *Bande Mataram* is sung the first two stanzas should be sung, with perfect freedom to the organizers to sing any other song of unobjectionable character, in addition to, or in place of *Bande Mataram* ."
6. Vijayalakshmi Pandit, addressee's sister.

---

79. Telegram to Jawaharlal Nehru

January 10, 1938

Mother lived nobly has died nobly. She was a model wife widow and mother. No sorrow. Let our women copy her example.

Love.

Bapu

80. Letter to Jawaharlal Nehru

Segaon,
April 25, 1938

My Dear Jawaharlal,

Here is a copy of Mahadev's notes on his Frontier Province visit. As I could not go and as we had disturbing news[1], I felt that he should be sent. I am not circulating the notes among all the members.

I am sending copies to the Maulana and Subhas. The notes have made me disconsolate. Mahadev has more to say. I am sending a copy, of course, to the Brothers[2]. I hope you will feel impelled to use your great influence over the Brothers. I am of course in telegraphic communication. I may even visit the Province for a few days, if Khan Saheb wants me to go, in spite of the shock I have received. We seem to be weakening from within. It hurts me that, at this very critical juncture in our history, we do not seem to see eye to eye in important matters. I can't tell you how positively lonely I feel to know that nowadays I can't carry you with me. I know that you would do much for affection. But in matters of state, there can be no surrender to affection, when the intellect rebels. My regard for you is deeper for your revolt. But that only intensifies the grief of loneliness. But I must stop.

Love.

Bapu

---

1. Presumably this is a reference to the tragedy at Mayar; *vide* "Speech at Mardan", 7-5-1938.
2. Khan Brothers.

---

81. Letter to Jawaharlal Nehru

On the Train to Peshawar,
April 30, 1938

My Dear Jawaharlal,

Here, is a copy of the brief notes I have jotted down of the 312 hours' talks with Jinnah. It may be that you and the other members may not like the basis. Personally, I see no escape from it. My handicap today is that I do not move about the country, as you do, and a still more serious handicap is the inner despondency that has overtaken me. I am carrying on, but it is galling to me to think that I have lost the self-confidence that I possessed only a month ago. I hope that this is but a temporary phase in my life. I have mentioned this to help you to examine the proposals on their merits. I do not suppose the first will present any difficulty. The second is novel, with all its implications. You will not hesitate summarily to reject it if it does not commend itself to you. In this matter you will have to give the lead.

I expect to return on the 11th. Subhas in reply to my telegram suggesting that he should open formal negotiations with Jinnah telegraphs that he will be in Bombay on the 10. I wish that you could also go there early. I am writing to Maulana Saheb in the same strain sending him a copy of this letter.

Love.

Bapu

---

82. Letter to Jawaharlal Nehru

May 7, 1938

My Dear Jawaharlal,

What is it in the new orientation of the Gandhi Seva Sangh that has disturbed you? I must own that I am responsible for it. I should like you to tell me unhesitatingly what has disturbed you. If I have erred, you know that I shall retrace my steps as soon as I discover the error.

As to the general deterioration, I agree with you, though we may differ as to the weak spots.

More when we meet.

Love.

Bapu

---

83. Letter to Jawaharlal Nehru

Segaon, Wardha,
May 26, 1938

My Dear Jawaharlal,

How very business-like and prompt you are ! I am so glad you were able to go into the Gurgaon D.C.C.'s affairs. I hope your advice will be accepted by both parties, as it should be.

Today, I have your letter about my notes of my talks with Jinnah.[1] I think my second talk with him was inevitable. I hope it won't do any harm. If you have time I would like you to give me a line about Jal after you have seen him. Now, I wish you will give yourself rest during your European tour and not rush as you have been doing here all the time.

Love.

Bapu

1. *Vide* "Letter to Jawaharlal Nehru", 30-4-1938.

84. Letter to Jawaharlal Nehru

Segaon, Wardha,
February 11, 1939

I have your wire and letter. I understand your position about the conference and the W.C. I cannot think of causes without the persons who handle them. I wrote about postponement on the strength of what I had heard from Balwantrai Mehta. He is engrossed in the Kathiawar struggle. Achintram could not do without him. So, I wired to you. I know nothing about the situation in Ludhiana.

I am sorry about Sarup. I was looking forward to her passing a few days with me.

Love.

Bapu

85. Telegram to Jawaharlal Nehru

Rajkot,
March 9, 1939

Jawaharlal Nehru
Tripuri Congress
[Jabalpur]

It will be first class blunder if resolution not taken to rid

Congress of internal corruption. Power should be given to A.I.C.C. to make required changes in Constitution without necessity their being submitted to Congress. Keeping well.[1]

Bapu

1. According to *The Hindu*, 11-3-1939, an identical telegram was sent to Subhas Chandra Bose. It was read out by Sarat Chandra Bose in the Subjects Committee meeting as the former could not attend it owing to bad health. Sarat Chandra Bose said that Subhas Chandra Bose "Whole-heartedly endorsed Gandhiji's view".

86. Letter to Jawaharlal Nehru

New Delhi,
March 30, 1939

My Dear Jawaharlal,

I had your two letters[1]. Both were good. I send you copies of correspondence. The events in U.P. disturb me.[2] My solution is that you should become Prime Minister or dissolve the Ministry. You must get control over the unruly elements.

I have had three days heart-to-heart conversations with the socialists who were here. Narendradev will report to you. If he does not of his own accord, you should make him.

Love.

Bapu

1. Dated March 22 and 24, forwarding copies of correspondence with Subhas Chandra Bose. Jawaharlal Nehru had also informed Gandhiji of his telegram to S.C. Bose that "...Gandhiji ...keenly feels Congress work suffering owing lack direction office arrangements also national, international crises demand ceaseless vigilance. . ." .
2. In "The Rajkot Fast–VIII", Pyarelal explains: "Communal riots in Allahabad exercise Gandhiji's mind very much." *Vide* also the following item.

87. Letter to Jawaharlal Nehru

New Delhi,
April 6, 1939

My Dear Jawaharlal,

Who can help feeling distressed over the turn things are taking?[1] Let us hope that the cloud would be soon lifted.

The Rajkot Award[2] is but one step towards the objective. I have still to watch the next step. However, I telephoned to Dr. Khan Sahib today. He has promised to telephone and tell me if he wants me. I was agitated over the raids that have become a feature there. I have to see the Viceroy today. I might have to go Rajkot in connection with the committee.

My love to Indu. I take it that Krishna[3] is also going. This means that you will be in Bombay on 15th?

Love.

Bapu

[P.S.]

I note what you say about the tension there.[4]

---

1. Jawaharlal Nehru, in his letter of April 1, had referred to a riot that broke out on March 29 at Baradari Hall, Lucknow, and had commented that communal riots were becoming political and superficial, with no passion or emotion about them. He thought that the local leaders of the Muslim League must be held responsible for what was happening.
2. *Vide* footnote 2, "Telegram to U.N. Dhebar", 3-4-1939.
3. Krishna Hutheesing addressee's sister.
4. The reference is to the communal tension in Allahabad.

88. Telegram to Jawaharlal Nehru

Delhi,
July 27, 1939

Jawaharlal Nehru
Care Congress
G[Irgaum], B[omba]Y

You Have Done Bravely and Spiritedly.[1]

Bapu

1. The addressee had just returned from his Ceylon tour. *Vide* also "Letter to Jawaharlal Nehru", 29-7-1939.

---

89. Letter to Jawaharlal Nehru

Segaon, Wardha,
July 29, 1939

My Dear Jawaharlal,

Instead of guiding the Dhami people I have passed them on to you.[1] I feel that you should discharge this burden without any interference from me. The idea in the States seems to be to isolate and ignore the Congress and hence the States Conference. I have already suggested[2] in *Harijan* that no State Association or Mandal should act on its own without reference to your committee[3]. I should act, if at all, through you; i.e., when you refer to me, I should give my opinion as I do in respect of the Working Committee. I told the Gwalior people also likewise yesterday. You will have to reorganize your committee a bit, if it is to function properly.

After all I could not go to Kashmir. Sheikh Abdullah and his friends won't tolerate the idea of my being State guest. Banking on my past experience, I had accepted State offer in anticipation of Sheikh Abdullah's approval. But I saw that I was mistaken. I therefore, cancelled the acceptance of the State hospitality and accepted the Sheikh's. This embarrassed the State. So, I cancelled the visit altogether.

I was guilty of double stupidity—in daring to think of going there without you and in not getting Sheikh's permission before accepting the State offer. I had thought that I would serve the people by accepting the State offer. I must confess that I was not pleased with my contact [with] the Sheikh and his friends. They seemed to all of us to be most unreasonable. Khan Saheb reasoned with them. But it was to no purpose.

Your visit to Ceylon was glorious. I don't mind what the immediate outcome is. Saleh Tyabji asks me to send you to Burma and Andrews thinks of you in connection with South Africa. For Ceylon the idea of a Congress deputation came to me spontaneously, not so these two even after the promptings. But of these when we meet. I hope you are fresh and that Krishna is enjoying herself.

Love.

Bapu

---

1. A deputation on behalf of the Himalayan States People's Conference met Gandhiji at Delhi on July 27, and apprised him of the firing in Dhami.
2. *Vide* "Minority Administration", 22-7-1939.
3. Standing Committee of All-India States Peoples's Conference, of which Jawaharlal Nehru was President.

90. Telegram to Jawaharlal Nehru

Wardha Ganj,
August 18, 1939

Jawaharlal Nehru
Anand Bhavan
Allahabad

May your Chinese Mission be crowned with success. May god be with you and bring you safe home. Regret Sri Prakasa. He should suspend action till after your Return.[1] Propose issuing a statement[2] on crisis and war resolution unless you wish otherwise. Send your Chinese address.

Love.

Bapu

---

1. Sri Prakasa wanted to resign from the Congress. *Vide* also "Telegram to Sri Prakasa", 26-8-1939.
2. *Vide* "A Statement", 20-9-1939.

91. Letter to Jawaharlal Nehru

Segaon, Wardha,
October 25, 1939

My Dear Jawaharlal,

I have gone through the American thing. It is most expensive. In other respects, too, it does not attract me.

I hope you have good news about Indu.[1]

Love.

Bapu

1. *Vide* footnote of "Letter to Indira Nehru", after 15-10-1939.

---

92. Letter to Jawaharlal Nehru

Segaon, Wardha
October 29, 1939

My Dear Jawaharlal,

I wrote to you yesterday. This is to send you a complaint from Meerut.[1] Please inquire and write directly to the correspondent. I have told him I have passed the letter on to you.

Love.

Bapu

1. The reference is, presumably, to the communal riots which broke out in Meerut on October 4, when the army was called out and arrests were made.

---

93. Letter to Jawaharlal Nehru

Railway Station, Delhi,
November 4, 1939

My Dear Jawaharlal,

Just after you had gone, Kripalani told me that in United Provinces there was great ferment and preparation for civil disobedience. He told me, too, that anonymous placards had been circulated asking people to cut wires and tear up rails. My own opinion is that there is at present no atmosphere for civil disobedience. If people take the law into their own hands I must give up command of civil disobedience movement. I would like you to read this week's *Harijan.*[1] It deals with my position in this connection.

It was this that I had intended to discuss with you. But it was not to be.

At this critical time in our history there should be no misunderstanding between us and, if possible, there should be one mind.

Love.

Bapu

1. *Vide* "The Next Step", 30-10-1939.

---

94. Letter to Jawaharlal Nehru

Segaon, Wardha,
November 14, 1939

My Dear Jawaharlal,

Your letters have been coming in regularly. I have seen yours to Rajen Babu. Before I saw it I had written a note[1] on it for *Harijan,* I must try to send you an advance copy.

If you need me longer in Allahabad, you will keep me.[2]

The interested editings in London of our statements here do not worry me. If I find time I shall write out a brief message[3] for *The News Chronicle.* I have prepaid authority from that paper.

More when we meet.

Love.

Bapu

[PS.]
Mahadev just reminds me that you complete half a century today. I hope you will complete the other half retaining the same vigour, frankness and robust honesty.

Bapu

1. The reference is, presumably, to the preceding item.

2. The addressee, in his letter dated November 8 to Gandhiji, said: "All the members of the U.P.P.C.C. were desirous of having an opportunity of meeting you, if this was possible during your stay in Allahabad.... The Working Committee is likely to last up to the 21st or possibly the 22nd. May I suggest the 23rd for an informal meeting between you and some of our prominent workers in the U.P., say, about 30 or so?"
3. *Vide* the following items.

---

95. Letter to Jawaharlal Nehru

Segaon, Wardha,
December 28, 1939

My Dear Jawaharlal,

I have your letter. I shall preserve the Chinese letter.[1]

The deliverance day[2] has received a full-page advertisement in *The T* [*imes*] *of I* [*ndia*]. But in truth, it seems to have fallen flat everywhere.

Have you read Fazlul Haq's indictment[3]? Should nothing be said or done about it?

You have not sent me Kumarappa's[4] letters to which you had raised strong objection. He is here. I asked him and he says he sent nothing recently. Do please send me what you may have.

Love.

Bapu

---

1. The addressee, in his letter dated December 25, had suggested that the letter from Chiang Kai-Shek might be preserved at Maganwadi. *Vide* "Letter to Chiang Kai- Shek", 5-1-1940.
2. *Vide* "Statement to the Press", 9-12-1939.
3. Presumably this refers to the Bengal Premier's speech in the Assembly on December 18, alleging that it was the majority, the Indian National Congress, that had stood in the way of India's political progress. "They are a selfish lot. They are dishonest."
4. J.C. Kumarappa, Secretary, A.I.V.I.A.

96. Letter to Jawaharlal Nehru

Segaon,
January 5, 1940

My Dear Jawaharlal,

Your letter makes me sad.[1] You said in indignant tones that Ku[marappa] was a worthless man. And this you did on the flimsiest testimony. I asked you for the correspondence and you said you had not it with you but would send it to me. Now I see you accepted the interpretation of others. My point is not that the interpretation was incorrect but that it was wrong to judge a co-worker on such hearsay.

I suggest your securing the correspondence and sending it to me.

Herewith my letter[2] to the Generalissimo. I have not released his to the Press. You will do so if you think it necessary.

Love.

Bapu

---

1. In his letter dated January 3, 1940, the addressee had written : "About Kumarappa's correspondence with the Planning Committee, I was told by Ambalal and Dr. Nazir Ahmad that they had approached him for certain information in regard to cottage industries and sought his co-operation on some other matters connected therewith. Both of them were very much hurt at the reply received from Kumarappa which seemed to them to refuse any kind of co-operation or help."
2. *Vide* the following item.

---

97. Letter to Jawaharlal Nehru

[After January 5, 1940][1]

My Dear Jawaharlal,

I have your letter. I know the possibility of misunderstandings.

These and ignorant or interested criticisms have never influenced me. I know that all would be well, if we are strong within. For the external affairs you are my guide. Your letter therefore helps me.

You have made more than ample amends about Kumarappa.

You will like to see his letter. You may destroy it after perusal. Yes, we have very few workers like him.

Love.

Bapu

1. From the reference to Kumarappa it is evident that this letter was written after the letter to the addressee dated January 5, 1940; *vide* "Letter to Jawaharlal Nehru", 5-1-1940.

98. Letter to Jawaharlal Nehru

Segaon, Wardha,
January 30, 1940

My Dear Jawaharlal,

Padma Pant of Cawnpore has sent me copy of his letter to you. I hope you will probe the truth.

Love.

Bapu

[PS.]
Have you seen the latest pamphlet of the Jamiat-Ulema-i-Hind? They are dangerous friends. I wonder if the W[orking] C[ommittee] had a full talk with Moulvi Kifayatulla Saheb !

99. Letter to Jawaharlal Nehru

On the Way to Delhi,
February 3, 1940

My Dear J.L.,

Read the within letter.[1] You know best what to do. These things require attention.

Love.

Bapu

1. Dr. Satyapal, in his letter to Rajendra Prasad dated January 24, described the communal activities of the Akalis and stated that "unless

the High Command includes these also in the list of communalists there is a grave danger of the Punjab Congress being entirely under the thumb of Akalis, and they will be a serious danger for this organization because of their being neither believers in truth, nor non-violence, nor nationalism …nor *Purna Swarajya*."

---

100. Letter to Jawaharlal Nehru

Segaon, Wardha,
[On or after February 7, 1940][1]

My Dear Jawaharlal,

I like your letter.[2] They give me information which I do not get otherwise. I knew nothing of the pan-Islamic movement.[3] It does not surprise me. You will have seen my statement[4] on the interview. My method you know. I gain strength from these meetings. It is for you and other co-workers to see that the country gets the proper interpretation of what I do. I would like you not to worry about C.R.[5] He is absolutely sound. Nevertheless I would like you to share your doubts with him. I leave for Santiniketan on 15th evening and thence on 19th for Malikanda.

Love.

Bapu

---

1. From the contents it is evident that this was written after Gandhiji's return to Segaon on February 7.
2. Both were dated February 4; *vide* "The Old Game?", 11-2-1940.
3. Regarding this the addressee had written : "I wonder if your attention has been drawn to a recent social function in London, organized by the Royal Central Asian Society. Lord Zetland presided and a number of Cabinet Ministers were present. The ostensible object was to establish a centre of Muslim culture and religion in London; the real object was to encourage pan-Islamism and to exploit this sentiment in India and in the Islamic countries to the advantage of the allies in the war."
4. *Vide* "Statement to the Press", 6-2-1940.
5. The addressee had expressed concern about some recent speeches of C. Rajagopalachari because "they talk so compromisingly of Dominion Status and the like".

---

101. Letter to Jawaharlal Nehru

Sevagram, Wardha,
May 23, 1940

My Dear Jawaharlal,

Read the enclosed and guide me. I have told the writer that his suggestion[1] attracts me and if I see my way clear I shall act up to it in part or wholly.

Love.

Yours,
Bapu

1. Abdul Hai Abbasi of Lucknow had suggested that since comunal troubles usually started in Northern India, Gandhiji should settle in a village in U.P. where Muslims were in a majority.

102. Letter to Jawaharlal Nehru

Sevagram, Wardha,
May 29, 1940

My Dear Jawaharlal,

I had your letter enclosing Mr. Spalding's. Thompson's was not in it. I am writing to S.[1] generally approving of your reply. That will save my time.

I have also yours enclosing reply to Sir Sikandar and your letter [to] the Maulana. Your statements are good and full. I purposely refrain from making statements. But I will when I find it necessary.

I hope you are having a good time in Kashmir.

Love.

Bapu

1. The letter to Spalding is not traceable.

103. Letter to Jawaharlal Nehru

Sevagram, Wardha,
July 15, 1940

My Dear Jawaharlal,

The idea about Urdu is good. You shall have a review of the Urdu writings by Hindus and of Urdu periodicals and books. There should be an Urdu weekly giving a dispassionate reply to the lies. It is uphill work to overtake deliberate lies but it is worth trying.

Love.

Bapu

Shri Jawaharlal Nehru
Lucknow, U.P.

---

104. Letter to Jawaharlal Nehru

Sevagram, Wardha,
August 8, 1940

My Dear Jawaharlal,

Maulana Saheb gave me the Hyderabad preliminary report. It makes fearful reading. There is nothing new in it for me. But one does not want confirmation of worst fears. I have been taxing myself about the remedy. I meet the workers tomorrow. If you have any thoughts pass them on to me.

Love.

Bapu

[PS.]
Will you send me any authentic evidence you may have of the war exactions?[1]

---

1. For Jawaharlal Nehru's reply, *vide* "Letter to Jawaharlal Nehru", 10-8-1940.

105. Letter to Jawaharlal Nehru

Sevagram, Wardha,
October 6, 1940

My Dear Jawaharlal,

I had your two letters.[1] You will tell me more about Rajni Patel when we meet. Your letter[2] about Napier[3], with enclosure, I am sending to the Viceroy. It is a pathetic case.

I am over head and ears in work. Hence, no more.

Love.

Bapu

1. One of these, dated September 21, was concerning the case of Rajni Patel, a barrister in Bombay, who had been arrested on his return after years of sojourn abroad.
2. Dated October 2, 1940; *vide* "Letter to Jawaharlal Nehru", 2-10-1940.
3. Great grandson of Sir Charles Napier.

106. Letter to Jawaharlal Nehru

Wardha,
October 21, 1940

My Dear Jawaharlal,

So, Vinoba has been fixed up. His four days' ministry has been quite successful from my point of view.

I am issuing a note[1] which you will see. Professor[2] telephoned saying you were ready. I have seen your statement too. I would still like to ask you whether you can see anything to commend itself to you in all I am writing and doing. I would not like you to go in merely as a disciplinarian. My present conception requires those who believe in the,plan—not in every detail but in the main. *Verb. sap.* Drop me a wire[3] if you can.

Love.

Bapu

1. *Vide* the preceding item.

2. J. B. Kripalani, General Secretary of the Congress.
3. In his telegram dated October 24, Jawaharlal Nehru said: "Your letter. Agree generally."

---

107. Letter to Jawaharlal Nehru

December 13, 1941

My Dear Jawaharlal,

I have your letter. I am glad Indu will be coming with you.

There is no winter worth the name here. The nights are cool, the days hot.

The questions we have to discuss are many. I trust you and Maulana Saheb will be here before the date of the Working Committee.

I have heavy meetings of the A.I.S.A. and G.S.S. beginning from 17th. I expect to finish all on 20th.

Sardar is bearing himself well.

Love.

Bapu

---

108. Letter to Jawaharlal Nehru

February 23, 1942

Chi. Jawaharlal,

Now, you may be a little free. What is to be done about the office of the States' People's [Conference]? And what about the journal? Pattabhi writes that he can publish the paper from Masulipatnam. His letter is enclosed. Dr. Menon is here. Balwantrai cannot take up the secretaryship. Nor can Jainarayan Vyas. Rangildas is available. Bapa does not like it. If the office is here, it can, of course, be kept going; but financial arrangements will have to be made.

Blessings from
Bapu

[PS.]
I hope you find no difficulty in deciphering my handwriting.

---

109. Letter to Jawaharlal Nehru

March 1, 1942

Chi. Jawaharlal,

I got your letter yesterday. I did not intend replying, nor do I want to do so now. I wish to remind you of the hot weather. The heat is severe. I am having a wet-pack on my head. Indu should not come this side during such heat. I would suggest that both of them should go to Khali or Kashmir. They should visit Sevagram and other places only after the rains. But if Indu has the courage to face the heat here, I shall, of course, be happy to meet the two.[1]

One thing more. Khurshedbehn had written to you. She says you have written to her that you are awaiting an invitation from the Mahatma. Why do you need an invitation from me? It is always there for you. There was no special work for which I should put you to the trouble of coming here. I do not understand the implications of an "open city", that is why I have said: "I must consult Jawaharlal before I say anything. I depend upon Jawaharlal in such matters."

We are meeting soon.

Blessings from
Bapu

1. Indira Nehru was engaged to Feroz Gandhi on February 26.

---

110. Letter to Jawaharlal Nehru

Sevagram, Wardha,
March 4, 1942

Chi. Jawaharlal,

Received your letter yesterday. Hope you will not find it difficult to read this letter.

About Indu's marriage, I hold the firm opinion that no one from outside need be invited. A few persons who are at Allahabad may, however, be called as witnesses. You can send invitation cards to as many people as you like. Ask for blessings from everybody but make it clear that no one in particular need take the trouble of coming. If one person is asked to come, others cannot be left out.

It has to be considered whether or not Indu likes to go to this extent of simplicity. In case you too do not like to go so far, you can rule out my suggestion.

I have seen your statement about Indu. I like it. I receive letters [concerning her marriage] everyday. Some are horrid. I have destroyed all of them. In reply to all these, I have sent a note in *Harijan*[1], a copy of which I am sending herewith. The note was written on Monday. Since, yesterday, letters from Muslims are pouring in, making Sarup the target of their attack. This will go on.

I will do all that is possible for the Indian States. Funds will be a constant difficulty. Jamnalalji had taken all the responsibility upon himself; how he would have done it was not decided. I am now wondering how to raise the money. I am consulting Pattabhi about the paper.[2] Balwantrai will not be able to come. That will not make much difference. We shall be getting help from here. When you come here, we shall talk over the matter. Menon is going to Bombay today to complete the work there.

I saw Chiang Kai-shek's statement. It was good. Your consent was received but I thought that there was no need now to make that letter public. The subject has become stale.

Bhagirathi has come. It is rather difficult to keep Chandra Singh. He is very much given to indulgence; and she is very weak.[3] He quarrels on petty matters. I will not be surprised if he beats up someone. I, however, find him hard-working. You need not worry. If you feel any difficulty in reading my letters, I will try to write more legibly. But it is our duty to start writing to each other in the national language. After some time we will find it easier to do so. The poor will be immensely benefited.

Blessings from
Bapu

1. *Vide* "Indira Nehru's Engagement", 2-3-1942.
2. *Vide* the following item.
3. A Bunch of Old Letters however has: "He is very much given to indulgence and has little intelligence".

111. Letter to Jawaharlal Nehru

Sevagram, Wardha,
March 9, 1942

Chi. Jawaharlal,

I have your letter. I had promptly replied to your earlier letter. I hope you got it.

Mukerji is a good and honest worker. He has some land. I had asked him. He said he did not seek charity. I have no doubt he will return the entire amount. He was prepared even to pay interest. We have given much aid to other workers. I am clearly of the view that we should lend Rs. 3,000 to Bhai Mukerji for six months.

Blessings from
Bapu

---

112. Letter to Jawaharlal Nehru

[After March 27, 1942*]*[1]

Chi. Jawaharlal,

Khurshedbehn is very unhappy. She feels that your heart has dried up towards her. Send for her, give her some affection. You know she adores you.[2]

Today I woke up at two. I was thinking of you and Rajaji only. I am clearly of the view that we cannot accept this 'offer'[3]. If you also agree, then talk to Rajaji and reach a final decision. If you are inclined to agree with Rajaji then the matter deserves further consideration.

Blessings from
Bapu

---

1. This was written on the back of a bill bearing this date. This is also confirmed by the reference to the "offer" brought by Sir Stafford Cripps. Gandhiji met him on March 27. *Vide* also Appendix "Interview with Sir Stanfford Cripps", 27-3-1942.
2. Gandhiji started writing this letter during massage. It appears from a dash in the source that the following paragraph was written some time later.

3. The British War Cabinet's proposals. *Vide* Appendix "British War Cabinet's Proposals", before 27-3-1942.

---

113. Letter to Jawaharlal Nehru

Sevagram, Wardha,
April 15, 1942

Chi. Jawaharlal,

The Professor is here. He has told me everything. I also heard about your Press interview. Whereas we have always had differences of opinion it appears to me that now we also differ in practice. What can Vallabhbhai and others do in such a situation? If your policy is accepted the Committee should not retain its present shape.

The more I think of it the more I feel that you are making a mistake. I see no good in American troops entering India and in our resorting to guerrilla warfare.

It is my duty to caution you.

I hope Indu and Feroze are well.

Blessings from
Bapu

[PS.]
I heard yesterday that the Forward Bloc people in Utkal are armed and that the Communists are ready for guerrilla warfare. I do not know how much truth there is in it.

---

114. Letter to Jawaharlal Nehru

Segaon, *Via* Wardha,
April 19, 1942

Chi. Jawaharlal,

A letter from the Maulana arrived today. He writes that I have to go to Allahabad. How can I go? I had said even when I was there that I was not any more fit for travel. And what shall I do by going there?

I have the same one thing to offer and I have called three meetings here. One of them has been planned for a long time. I cannot miss any of them. You must therefore excuse me. Write to Maulana to spare me.

Blessings from
Bapu

[PS.]
Janakibehn wrote to you yesterday to hold both the meetings at Wardha. I withheld the letter. Meetings should be held at Wardha when my presence is considered essential.

---

115. Letter to Jawaharlal Nehru

Sevagram, Wardha,
April 24, 1942

Chi. Jawaharlal,

Mirabehn agrees that I must take some step and that she will have to make a sacrifice. She wanted to go to Allahabad[1] even if I did not go. I have therefore called her here. I am sending through her my views in the form of a resolution[2]. Maulana Saheb has been urging me to go to Allahabad. I have told him, I am helpless. I find travelling difficult these days. What is more, I have called three meetings for the same period. I have therefore asked Maulana Saheb to excuse me and told him that I shall be sending my views in the form of a resolution.

I do not think it necessary to give arguments in support of the resolution. If you do not like my resolution, I really cannot insist. The time has come when each of us must choose his own course.

The behaviour of the Government in Feni and other places is simply intolerable. What will such a Government do even if it survives? And today it is only trying to save itself. I am now certain that if this Government goes we shall be well able to deal with Japan. It is another matter that after the Government is removed we may fight among ourselves. Even if that should be so, do we want to save ourselves from internal quarrels through the good offices of this Government?

Acharya Narendra Dev has seen the resolution and liked it.

Blessings from
Bapu

---

116. Letter to Jawaharlal Nehru

Sevagram, Wardha,
May 9, 1942

Chi. Jawaharlal,

I have been awaiting your letter everyday. It has arrived today.

You do need a little rest. Many people have given me reports of Indu's work. She will become perfectly fit if she always maintains good health.

They tell me also that Feroze too is doing good work.

Everything possible is being done for Chandra Singh. Madhavi has got whooping cough. I visit her everyday. Chandra Singh and Bhagirathi appear happy. They do not complain much about the heat now. The problem of Chandra Singh's education is difficult. I am going to Bombay for eight days in connection with the Deenbandhu Memorial. I shall do whatever I can on my return. You should not worry.

Maulana's letters come regularly. He too is unwell. He writes to say that he will be coming to Wardha towards the end of this month.

Perhaps you too will be coming along with him?

Ba is well.

Blessings to both from
Bapu

---

117. Letter to Jawaharlal Nehru

Sevagram, Wardha,
June 5, 1942

Chi. Jawaharlal,

I received your letter.

There is nothing from Maulana. In one letter he had said that he would be accompanying you here.

Fischer[1] has arrived. I do manage to give him an hour everyday. He is staying at the Ashram.

Hot winds are blowing here.

Blessings from
Bapu

1. Louis Fischer. For an account of his talks with Gandhiji, *vide* Appendix, "Interview with Louis Fischer", 4-6-1942.

---

118. Letter to Jawaharlal Nehru

Sevagram, Wardha,
July 13, 1942

Chi. Jawaharlal,

I have read the resolution. I note that you have tried to include some of my points. I do not desire any modification.

But I do desire that, as far as possible, all of us should interpret the appeal in the same way. It will not be good if we speak in different voices.

I stick to the hundred per cent support I gave you in what you said about yourself. I have thought over the matter a great deal and still feel that your capacity for service will increase if you withdraw.

And to that extent you will find satisfaction. You may attend the Committee occasionally as I do or as Narendra Dev does. This will ensure your help being available and at the same time your fully retaining your freedom.

This is my plea about Maulana Saheb. I find that the two of us have drifted apart. I do not understand him nor does he understand me. We are drifting apart on the Hindu-Muslim question as well as on other questions. I have also a suspicion that Maulana Saheb does not entirely approve of the proposed action. No one is at fault. We have to face the facts. Therefore, I suggest that the Maulana should relinquish Presidentship but remain in the Committee, the Committee should elect an interim President and all should proceed unitedly. This great struggle cannot be conducted properly without unity and without a President who comes forth with a hundred per cent co-operation.

Please show this letter to Maulana Saheb. At the moment it is intended for you two only. If you do not like either or both of my suggestions, you may reject them. My motive in writing this is only to help. Whether you approve of it or not, it should not cause any unpleasantness.

The date and venue for the A.I.C.C. have not been indicated in your draft.

As far as I am concerned, you are free to issue this appeal to the Press.

It is not necessary to come here for a discussion of the resolution. But it has to be as Maulana Saheb orders.

Blessings from
Bapu

---

119. Letter to Jawaharlal Nehru

Sevagram,
August 8, 1945

Chi. Jawaharlal,

Your letter is beautiful. Come back fully recovered Indu has done a bold thing. I have written to Menon[1]. I enclose a copy. That is all the time I can spare.

Blessings from
Bapu

From a copy of the Hindi: Pyarelal Papers. *Courtesy*: Pyarelal

1. *Vide* the preceding item.

---

120. Letter to Jawaharlal Nehru

October 5, 1945

Chi. Jawaharlal,

I have long been intending to write to you but can do so only today. I have also been wondering whether I should write in English or Hindustani. In the end I have decided to write in Hindustani.

I take first the sharp difference of opinion that has arisen between us. If such a difference really exists people should also know about it, for the work of *swaraj* will suffer if they are kept in the dark.

I have said that I fully stand by the kind of governance which I have described in *Hind Swaraj*.[1] It is not just a way of speaking. My experience has confirmed the truth of what I wrote in 1909.[2] If I were the only one left who believed in it, I would not be sorry. For I can only testify to the truth as I see it. I have not *Hind Swaraj* in front of me. It is better that I redraw the picture today in my own language.

Then it would not matter to me whether or not the picture tallies with that of 1909[3], nor should it to you. I do not have to establish what I had said before. What is worth knowing is only what I have to say today. I believe that if India, and through India the world, is to achieve real freedom, then sooner or later we shall have to go and live in the villages—in huts, not in palaces. Millions of people can never live in cities and palaces in comfort and peace. Nor can they do so by killing one another, that is, by resorting to violence and untruth. I have not the slightest doubt that, but for the pair, truth and non-violence, mankind will be doomed. We can have the vision of that truth and non-violence only in the simplicity of the villages. That simplicity resides in the spinning-wheel and what is implied by the spinning wheel.

It does not frighten me at all that the world seems to be going in the opposite direction. For the matter of that, when the moth approaches its doom it whirls round faster and faster till it is burnt up.

It is possible that India will not be able to escape this moth-like circling. It is my duty to try, till my last breath, to save India and through it the world from such a fate. The sum and substance of what I want to say is that the individual person should have control over the things that are necessary for the sustenance of life. If he cannot have such control the individual cannot survive. Ultimately, the world is made up only of individuals. If there were no drops there would be no ocean. This is only a rough and ready statement. There is nothing new in this.

But even in *Hind Swaraj* I have not said all this. While I appreciate modern thought, I find that an ancient thing, considered in the light of this thought looks so sweet. You will not be able to understand me if you think that I am talking about the villages of today. My ideal village still exists only in my imagination.

After all every human being lives in the world of his own imagination. In this village of my dreams the villager will not be dull—he will be all awareness. He will not live like an animal in filth and darkness. Men and women will live in freedom, prepared to face the whole world. There will be no plague, no cholera and no smallpox. Nobody will be allowed to be idle or to wallow in luxury. Everyone will have to do body labour. Granting all this, I can still envisage a number of things that will have to be organized on a large scale. Perhaps there will even be railways and also post and telegraph offices. I do not know what things there will be or will not be. Nor am I bothered about it. If I can make sure of the essential thing, other things will follow in due course. But if I give up the essential thing, I give up everything.

The other day, at the final day's meeting of the Working Committee, we had taken a decision to the effect that the Working Committee would meet for two or three days to work out this very thing. I shall be happy if it meets. But even if it does not meet, I want that we two should understand each other fully. And this for two reasons. Our bond is not merely political. It is much deeper. I have no measure to fathom that depth. This bond can never be broken. I therefore want that we should understand each other thoroughly in politics as well. The second reason is that neither of us considers himself as worthless. We both live only for India's freedom, and will be happy to die too for that freedom. We do not care for praise from any quarter. Praise or abuse are the same to us. They have no place in the mission of service. Though I aspire to live up to 125 years rendering service, I am nevertheless an old man, while you are comparatively young. That is why I have said that you are my heir.[4] It is only proper that I should at least understand my heir and my heir in turn should understand me. I shall then be at peace.

One thing more. I had written to you[5] about Kasturba Trust and Hindustani. You had said you would write after thinking things over. I find that your name is already figuring in the Hindustani Sabha.

Nanavati reminded me that he had approached you and Maulana Saheb and that you had appended your signature. That was in 1942.

That was long ago. You know where Hindustani stands today. If you still stand by that signature, I wish to get some work out of you in this regard. It will not involve much running about, but some work will be called for.

The work of Kasturba Memorial Trust is rather complicated. I realize that if what I have said above is going to irk you or is irking you, you will not feel comfortable even in the Kasturba Trust.

The last point concerns the sparks that are flying about in the conflict with Sarat Babu.[6] I have been pained by the episode. I have been unable to trace it to its root. If what you have told me is all there is to it and nothing more remains to be said, then I do not have to inquire further. But if an explanation seems necessary, I very much want to hear it.

If we have to meet to thrash out all these matters, then we should find time for a meeting.

You are working very hard. I trust you are in good health and Indu[7] is well.

Blessings from
Bapu

---

1. *Vide "Hind Swaraj"*.
2. The source however has "1908".
3. *Ibid.*
4 *Vide* also "Speech at A.I.I.C. Meeting", 15-1-1942.
5. *Vide* "Letter to Jawaharlal Nehru", 25-6-1945.
6. *Vide* footnote 1, "Letter to Sarat Chandra Bose", 5-10-1945.
7. Indira, addressee's daughter.

---

121. Letter to Jawaharlal Nehru

Panchgani,
July 17, 1946

Chi. Jawaharlal,

I have gone through what Munshi showed me,[1] though I did not have the time to examine it closely. He came today after 4 O'clock and will be going back tomorrow morning. I had a long talk with him about grouping. He will explain things to you. I have advised him to consult other lawyers as well. What he has prepared after seven days' labours may not be placed before the Committee just yet. Once it goes before the Committee, it will become public. I do not see the need of making it public so soon.

Your statement as published in the papers does not sound good.[2] If it is correctly reported, some explanation is needed. It must be admitted that we have to work within the limits of the State Paper. It is clear in Maulana's letters. We have given it our own interpretation.

But if the Federal Court gives a different interpretation, we shall have to be firm. I think it necessary to say this clearly. If we do not admit even this much, we will be doing nothing and Jinnah Saheb's accusation will prove true.

Fischer[3] and Jayaprakash have come here today. They too will return tomorrow.

Blessings from
Bapu

[PS.]
In regard to Kashmir, Sardar has sent me the Maharaja's speech. It deserves careful study. I think a meeting of the Working Committee should be called to consider it. Let us not be hasty. Let us not endanger the whole thing just for this reason. I am of the view that Maulana Saheb and, if necessary, Sardar too, should go to Kashmir.
After all, has not the Working Committee assumed the entire responsibility?

Bapu

---

1. The reference is to the Rules of Procedure in the Constituent Assembly.
2. The reference is presumably to Jawaharlal Nehru's Press Statement of July 10, 1946, in which he had said that the Congress would enter the Constituent Assembly "completely unfettered by agreements and free to meet all situations as they arise".
3. Louis Fischer.

122. Telegram to Jawaharlal Nehru

July 19, 1946

Your wire[1] sent letter yesterday. Just received letter from Minister enclosing copy Maharaja's letter to you. I consider that letter satisfies minimum demand. After finishing work Delhi you should go Kashmir taking Maulana if he will come. Inform Maharaja of date departure telling him you are aware of ban on meeting and demonstrations adding you have no desire to do more than meeting Sheikh Abdullah and attending to his defence. Keep me informed of your movements.

---

1. Dated July 18, 1946, this read : "Have received no communication from Kashmir. In view Maharaja's recent speech as reported no change in policy indicated.
Please advise about future action. Am going Delhi tomorrow."

---

123. Letter to Jawaharlal Nehru

Harijan Colony,
New Delhi,
August 29, 1946

Chi. Jawaharlal,

We never have a moment to ourselves. I do not ask for it. You never have any time to spare. Nor do I have any. So, a good many matters remain untouched.

I have before me your letter of the 20th. It came to me yesterday *via* Wardha. It dwells on the question of who should be the Congress President in view of the fact that you will be the Prime Minister. You incline in favour of Maulana Saheb. This I do not understand and cannot understand. In my view, Maulana Saheb should not accept nomination. Maulana Saheb hesitates to accept ministership. The responsibilities of the President, especially in the present juncture, are I feel arduous. But in my view it is not the only reason why he should not be president. I cannot accept, too, that other than Maulana Saheb, Sardar Patel and Rajendra Babu, no suitable person can be found.

I cannot definitely say who else will be suitable because I am not any more in very close with the Congress organization.

One thing more. It is also a question as to who should be the President of the Constituent Assembly. I shall not write anything more about it now, because it is not certain whether the Constituent Assembly will meet. Once the Working Committee meeting is over I do not think it is necessary for me to stay on here or at Mussoorie.

This hardly needs to be discussed at the Working Committee. Please consider and tell me what I should do. I shall do as you say.

Blessings from
Bapu

[PS.]
I have a great deal of work to do at Wardha. You may show this whole letter to Maulana Saheb.

---

124. Letter to Jawaharlal Nehru

New Delhi,
September 3, 1946

Chi. Jawaharlal,

Dr. Shaukatullah Ansari[1], who was here yesterday, tells me that your health is deteriorating and that there is fear of a nervous breakdown. People say that you keep working till past midnight. I am certain this is not at all good. For the work ahead of you, you need great care. This becomes impossible if you overstrain your mental resources.

Blessings from
Bapu

---

1. Son-in-law of Dr. M.A. Ansari.

125. Letter to Jawaharlal Nehru

November 5, 1946

Chi. Jawaharlal,

The events in Bihar have distressed me. I can clearly see my duty. My bonds with Bihar are close. I cannot forget it. If half of what I hear is true, it means that Bihar has lost all humanity. To say that *goondas* were responsible for whatever happened there would be quite untrue. Although I have tried hard to avoid the fast, I shall not be able to do so. It is the seventh day today since I gave up milk and cereals. The cough and the boils were responsible for it, but also I was tired of the body. Then Bihar made matters worse. And the cry came from within: "Why should you be a witness to this slaughter?"

If your word, which is as clear as daylight, is not heeded, your work is over. Why do you not die? Such reasoning has forced me to resort to fasting. I want to issue a statement that if in Bihar and other provinces slaughter is not stopped, I must end my life by fasting.

The letter Mohammed Yunus wrote to Shamsuddin[1] is with Sardar Baldev Singh.[2] See it. Is what it says correct? It is our duty to give full report of what happened.

My low diet will continue. There may be delay in undertaking the fast. In Delhi you had asked me about the fast.

I had said I had no idea then. Now, the situation is not the same.

Still you may say what you want to say. If it appeals to me I shall give up the idea of a fast. What I hope is that, knowing my nature, you will appreciate my position. Whatever the issue, I shall advise that all of you continue to do your work. Do not waste time thinking of my death. Leave me in the hands of God and stop worrying.

You can show this letter to the Bihar Cabinet. Is this the Bihar of Brijkishore Prasad?[3]

Blessings from
Bapu

---

1. Shamsuddin Ahmed, Minister of Commerce, Labour and Industries in the Bengal Muslim League Ministry.

2. Minister of Defence in the Interim Government.
3. A Congress leader of Bihar: Father-in-law of Jayaprakash Narayan.

---

126. Letter to Jawaharlal Nehru

Kazirkhil,
Ramganj P.S.,
Noakhali Distt.,
January 30, 1947

Dear Jawaharlal,

I have yours of the 20th instant about Shri Bhargava's offer[1] from Katni. The gentleman wrote to me probably at the same time that he wrote to you and I replied promptly. I cannot lay my hands on a copy of what I wrote. But the purport was that there would be no ladies [willing] to go so far. I think I told him also that I did not like his laying stress upon Hindus.

In my wandering I did not find that there is any inclination on the part of the sufferers to go out of Bengal. Nor do I think it wise. For it they cannot, out of fright, return to their village homes, they will all be accommodated in other parts of Bengal. A large number are already in Assam. Some have gone to Bihar because there is a large Bengali settlement there. My own effort is to send them to their villages, to make them shed all fear and to dissuade them from forsaking their ancestral homes. Nevertheless, if there are any who would like to go to Katni, of which there seems to be no likelihood, I would of course bear Shri Bhargava's offer in mind.

Blessings from
Bapu

---

1. B. K. Bhargava had made an offer to maintain and find a home for a 100 to 200 Hindu families from East Bengal.

---

127. Letter to Jawaharlal Nehru[1]

February 6, 1947

I know that if I were free I could take my share in trying to solve the various problems that arise in our country. But I feel that I should be useless unless I could do something here.... We are all in the hands of Power which we call God.

***

Very great pressure is being put upon me to go to Bihar because they all say that things are not properly represented to me on behalf of the Bihar Government. I am watching.

1. Nehru in his letter dated January 30, 1947, had written : "I know that we must learn to rely upon ourselves and not run to you for help on every occasion. But we have got into this bad habit and we do often feel that if you had been easier of access, our difficulties would have been less." *Vide* also "Extract from Letter to Abul Kalam Azad", 12-2-1947.

128. Letter to Jawaharlal Nehru

February [26][1], 1947

The last week of March next is at present for me a far cry. If God wills He will find a way for me to attend the Conference.[2]

1. The source has "6", obviously a slip, since this letter was in reply to the addressee's letter dated February 24, soliciting Gandhiji's presence at the Inter-Asian Relations Conference which was to be held in New Delhi from March 23.
2. Gandhiji ultimately did attend the Conference on April 1 and 2.

129. Letter to Jawaharlal Nehru

April 18, 1947

Chi. Jawaharlal,

Who will now sign the cheques concerning the Jallianwala

Bagh[1] since Malaviyaji[2] is no more? As the Sardar happens to be there, consult him and let me know.

Blessing from
Bapu

[From Hindi]

1. Jallianwala Bagh Memorial Trust.
2. Madan Mohan Malaviya.

130. Letter to Jawaharlal Nehru

June 7, 1947[1]

I had a long conversation with His Excellency....[1] The more I see His Excellency the more I feel that he is sincere. But it is quite possible to damage him if the surrounding atmosphere of which the Indian element is the author overwhelms him as it may well do any of us.

All the points we discussed[2] at the Working Committee meeting yesterday were touched upon by me and I carried with me the impression that he really appreciated them.

To be wholly truthful requires the highest form of bravery and therefore of non-violence.

1. Omission as in the source.
2. *Vide* "Notes for Discussion with Viceroy", 6-6-1947.

131. Letter to Jawaharlal Nehru

June 7, 1947

The oftener we meet the more convinces I am becoming that the gulf between us in the thought world is deeper than I had feared. He (the Sardar)[1] says that you are largely responsible for the present situation. He is of the opinion that Badshah Khan's....[2] influence is on the wane. Badshah Khan has not left any such impression on me.

Whatever he is today, he was always. There is undoubtedly more steadiness today than before. I also feel that Dr. Khan Saheb[3] and his colleagues would be nowhere without the Badshah. He alone counts in so far as the Congress influence is concerned.

If the Qaid-e-Azam does not go to the Frontier and does not woo the Badshah, his brother and his other colleagues, the Frontier Ministry should resign and so also the Parliamentary majority on the sole ground that a referendum at this moment must lead to bloodshed and probably, if not certainly, to a lasting blood-feud, which they should avoid in so far as it is humanly possible. Amrit (Rajkumari Amrit Kaur) tells me that you think to the contrary. You think the referendum should take place now.... You are also of opinion that a referendum will not cause bloodshed, indeed that my proposal would be more likely to cause it. I do not share this view. I had told the Badshah that if I do not carry you with me. I shall retire at least from the Frontier consultation and let you guide him. I will and cannot interpose myself between you and him. After all, was it not you who brought him to me? You will now decide and tell me.

---

1. Vallabhbhai Patel had an hour's talk with Gandhiji on the night of June 6.
2. Omissions as in the source.
3. Prime Minister of N.W.F.P., brother of Abdul Ghaffar Khan.

---

132. Draft of Letter to Jawaharlal Nehru

June 9, 1947[1]

Chi. Jawaharlal,[2]

I have your note which I have read most carefully. If I shared your premises, I should whole-heartedly agree with you.

I am sending your note by messenger to the Badshah with my covering letter[3] of which I enclose a copy herewith.

The more I contemplate the differences in outlook and opinion between the members of the W. C. and me, I feel that my presence is unnecessary even if it is not detrimental to the cause we all have at heart. May I not go back to Bihar in two or three days?

Would it be wrong if you insisted that referendum would be wrong without the presentation of the picture of Pakistan?[4]

---

1. From the source.
2. The superscription in Devanagari is not in Gandhiji's hand.
3. *Vide* the preceding item.
4. Omission as in the source.

---

133. Letter to Jawaharlal Nehru

New Delhi,
June 30, 1947

Chi. Jawaharlal[1],

Your letter. I have the invitation. I shall be at the Viceroy's house at 10 a. m. tomorrow. You or Vallabhbhai can fetch me, if that will save petrol.

Blessings from[2]
Bapu

[PS.]
I spoke at the meeting about B[adshah] Khan.[3]

---

1. The superscription and subscription are in Hindi.
2. *Ibid.*
3. *Vide* "Speech at Prayer Meeting", 30-6-1947.

---

134. Letter to Jawaharlal Nehru

July 24, 1947

Chi. Jawaharlal[1],

I did not say anything yesterday about the Maulana Saheb. But my objection stands. His retiring from the cabinet should not affect our connection with him. There are many positions which he can occupy in public life without any harm to any cause. Sardar is decidedly against his membership in the cabinet and so is Rajkumari.

Your cabinet must be strong and effective at the present juncture. It should not be difficult to name another Muslim for the cabinet.

I have destroyed the two copies you sent me yesterday.

Blessings from
Bapu

---

1. The superscription and the subscription are in Hindi.

---

135. Letter to Jawaharlal Nehru

August 29, 1947

Herewith is a letter from one Sardar Ajit Singh. You will see he is insistent on my going to the Punjab without a moment's delay. You will judge what I should do. Will it be any use my going after life and property are destroyed to the saturation point? Will it not be a mockery? I put before you for consideration the thoughts welling up within me. I have three wires pressing me to go.[1]

---

1. The addressee wired his reply the same day saying: "I still think that time has not come for you to visit the Punjab but feel your presence in Delhi very desirable so as to keep in touch with the Punjab situation and advise us."

---

136. Letter to Jawaharlal Nehru

August 30, 1947

About my going to the Punjab, I won't move without your and Vallabhbhai's wish. I want to say, however, that everyday pressure is being put upon me to rush to the Punjab before it is too late. If you wish I could send you all that comes to me so as to enable you to come to the right decision.

If I am not going to the Punjab, would I be of much use in Delhi as an adviser or consultant? I fancy I am not built that way. My advice has value only when I am actually working at a particular thing. I can only disturb when I give academic advice as on food, clothing, the use of the military. The more I think, the more I sense the truth of this opinion. Left to myself I would probably rush to the Punjab and if necessary break myself in the attempt to stop the warring elements from committing suicide. From a letter I just have from Lord Mountbatten I get the same impression.[1] He would welcome my immediate going to the Punjab.

On this side I have work which must help you all.

1. *Vide* the preceding item.

137. Telegram to Jawaharlal Nehru

New Delhi
[On or before September 7, 1947][1]

Pandit Nehru

God Willing Leaving for Delhi Way Punjab.
Inform Sardar Birla[2] Brijkrishna[3].

Bapu

From a facsimile: *Mahatma*, Vol. VIII, between pp. 152 and 153.

1. Gandhiji left Calcutta for Delhi on September 7.
2. G. D. Birla.
3. Brijikrishna Chandiwala.

138. Note to Jawaharlal Nehru

[September 29, 1947][1]

So far as the war is concerned my speeches have been quite clear. The summaries sent to America and elsewhere may be quite the contrary of what I might have said. I shall deal with the question more fully in my written speech today. As to the deteriorating situation I have told you quite firmly that you should dispense with Sardar, or he you. He won't shoulder the burden without you, hence you should take it up and reform the Cabinet with one mind. Rajen Babu should give up food portfolio. He will do so gladly.

I have always looked upon the wholesale accessions of States with suspicion. They are probably a liability rather than an asset. This sums up my reaction. We may discuss these things more fully when I can speak.

Jawaharlal Nehru Papers (Undated). *Courtesy*: Nehru Memorial Museum and Library.

---

1. From the reference to the "written speech today" in which Gandhiji clarified his stand on the war; *vide* "Speech at Prayer Meeting", 29-9-1947.

PART TWO
Jawaharlal Nehru's Letters to Mahatma Gandhi

Jawaharlal Nehru's Letters to Mahatma Gandhi

2.1 Letter from Jawaharlal Nehru[1]

Allahabad,
January 11, 1928

My Dear Bapuji,

The Working Committee is now meeting in Banaras and so I cannot go to Bombay or Sabarmati for some time.

I am loath to inflict another letter on you so soon after my last but I am very much troubled by your criticisms of the Congress resolutions and I feel I must write to you again. You are always very careful with you words and your language is studiously restrained. It amazes me all the more to find you using language which appears to me wholly unjustified. You have condemned in general language the proceedings of the Subjects Committee and specially selected some resolutions for greater criticism and condemnation. May I point out that it is always unsafe to judge on hearsay evidence? You were not present yourself and it is quite conceivable that the opinions you may have formed after a personal visit to the Subjects Committee may have been different. Yet you have chosen to condemn and judge unfavourably the whole Committee, or at any rate a great majority of it, simply basing your judgement on the impressions of a few persons. Do you think this is quite fair to the Committee or the Congress? You have referred to discipline and to the Working Committee as the National Cabinet. May I remind you that you are a member of the Working Committee and it is an extraordinary thing for a member on the morrow of the Congress to criticize, and run down the Congress and its principal resolutions. There has been a general chorus of congratulation on the success of the Madras Congress. This may be wrong or without sufficient basis but undoubtedly there was this general impression in the country and atmosphere counts for a great deal in all public work. And now most people who thought so feel a bit dazed at your criticisms and wonder if their previous enthusiasm was not overdone or mistaken.

You have described the Independence Resolution as "hastily conceived and thoughtlessly passed". I have already pointed out to you how the country has discussed and considered this question for years past, and how I have personally thought over it, discussed it, spoken about it in meetings, written about it and generally been full of it for the last five years or more. It seems to me that under the circumstances no stretch of language can justify the use of the words "hastily conceived". As for "thoughtlessly passed" I wonder if you know that the resolution was discussed in the Subjects Committee for about three hours and more than a dozen speeches for and against were made. Ultimately, as you know it was passed almost unanimously both in the Committee and the open Congress. Were all the people in the Committee and the Congress who voted for it "thoughtless"? Is this not rather a large assumption? And why should it not be said with greater truth that the small minority opposed to the resolution were mistaken? You mention that last year the resolution was rejected by the Committee. I do not know what inference you draw from this but to me it seems obvious that this can only mean that the Committee and the Congress have been eager to pass it in the past as in the present but refrained from doing so out of regard for you. I hope will agree with me that it is not healthy politics for any organization to subordinate its own definite opinion on a public issue out of personal regard only.

I am not referring here to the merits of the resolution. But I shall only say this that after prolonged and careful thought a demand for independence and all that this implies has come to mean a very great deal for me and I attach more importance to it than to almost anything else. I have thought over every word you said the other day in Madras on this question and it has merely confirmed me in my opinion. But I doubt if anyone outside a small circle understands your position in regard to this. I am sure that none of the others—liberals etc.,— who want dominion status think in the same way with you. Yesterday Sir Ali Imam addressed a meeting here on the Simon boycott. I also spoke for a few minutes and like King Charles' head independence cropped up and I laid stress on it. After the meeting Ali Imam told me that I did well in laying stress on this; he and his friends would probably come round to this position sooner or later but for the time being they had to be a little restrained as they wanted to carry many people with them. I am sure most liberals welcome the Independence Resolution, whatever they may say about it, as they feel that it strengthens their position. But whether they like it or not, it passes my comprehension how a national organization can have as its ideal and goal dominion status. The very idea suffocates and strangles me.

I took no special interest in the resolution on the boycott of British goods chiefly because I felt that it would meet with your strong disapproval and the boycott could not succeed unless a more or less unanimous effort was made. But I have no doubt that it can be made into a partial success if there was some unanimity in our own ranks. You must have read about the wonderful effectiveness of the boycott in China.

There was nothing special in China which we have not got and there is no fundamental reason why we cannot succeed where they succeeded. But granting that it is not likely to succeed is it such a laughing matter after all? Has our boycott of foreign cloth by *khaddar* succeeded so remarkably? Has our spinning franchise succeeded? They have not but you do not hesitate to them on the country and the Congress because you felt, and rightly, that they would be good for the nation even if they did not wholly succeed.

I remember how Kelkar, Aney and Co., even as members of the Working Committee, used to make fun of the Congress resolutions on *khudi*, and it is very painful for me to think that you are also ridiculing important Congress resolutions.

The Kelkars and Aneys do not count and I do not care what they say or do. But I do care very much for what you say and do.

Having singled out two resolutions for your special condemnation you casually refer to the others as "several irresponsible resolutions". Excepting the Unity Resolution every other resolution of the Congress may come under this heading. And so the labours of the 200 and odd persons in the Subjects Committee and the larger number in the Congress are summarily and rather contemptuously disposed of. It is very hard luck on the unhappy persons who, though wanting perhaps in foresight and intelligence, did not spare themselves and tried to do their best. We have all sunk to the level of the schoolboys' 'debating society' and you chastize us like an angry schoolmaster, but a schoolmaster who will not guide us or give us lessons but will only point out from time-to-time the error of our ways. Personally, I very much wish that we were more like real schoolboys, with the life and energy and daring of schoolboys, and a little less like the right honourable and honourable gentlemen who are for ever weighing the pros and cons and counting the cost.

You know how intensely I have admired you and believed in you as a leader who can lead this country to victory and freedom. I have done so in spite of the fact that I hardly agreed with anything that some of your previous publications—*Indian Home Rule* etc.,—contained. I felt and feel that you were and are infinitely greater than your little books. Above everything I admire action and daring and courage and I found them all in you in a superlative degree. And I felt instinctively that, however much I may disagree with you, your great personality and your possession of these qualities would carry us to our goal. During the N.C.O. period you were supreme; you were in your element and automatically you took the right step. But since you came out of prison something seems to have gone wrong and you have been very obviously ill at ease. You will remember how within a few months or even weeks you repeatedly changed your attitude—the Juhu statements, the A.I.C.C. meeting at Ahmedabad and after etc.,—and most of us were left in utter bewilderment. That bewilderment has continued since then. I have asked you many times what you expected to do in the future and your answers have been far from satisfying. All you have said has been that within a year or eighteen months you expected the *khadi* movement to spread rapidly and in a geometric ratio and then some direct action in the political field might be indulged in. Several years and eighteen months have passed since then and the miracle has not happened. It was difficult to believe that it would happen but faith in your amazing capacity to bring off the improbable kept us in an expectant mood. But such faith for an irreligious person like me is a poor reed to reply on and I am beginning to think if we are to wait for freedom till *khadi* becomes universal in India we shall have to wait till the Greek Kalends. *Khadi* will grow slowly, and if war comes it will grow very fast, but I do not see how freedom is coming in its train. As I mentioned before you our *khadi* work is almost wholly divorced from politics and our *khadi* workers are developing a mentality which does not concern itself with anything outside their limited sphere of work. This may be good for the work they do, but little can be expected from them in the political field.

What then can be done? You say nothing,—you only criticize and no helpful lead comes from you. You tell us that if the country will not even take to *khadi* how can we expect it to do anything more difficult or daring. I do not think the reasoning is correct. If the country does not go ahead politically by one method, surely it is up to our leaders to think of other or additional methods.

Reading many of your articles in *Young India*—your autobiography etc., —I have often felt how very different my ideals were from yours. And I have felt that you were very hasty in your judgements, or rather having arrived at certain conclusions you were over-eager to justify them by any scrap of evidence you might get. I remember how in an article on the "Two Ways" or some such title—you gave some newspaper cuttings from America about crimes and immorality and contrasted American civilization with Indian. I felt it was something like Katharine Mayo drawing conclusions from some unsavoury hospital statistics. Your long series of articles based on the French book—"Towards Moral Bankruptcy"—also made me feel the same way. You misjudge greatly, I think, the civilization of the West and attach too great an importance to its many failings. You have stated somewhere that India has nothing to learn from the West and that she had reached a pinnacle of wisdom in the past. I certainly disagree with this viewpoint and I neither think that the so-called *Ramaraj* was very good in the past, nor do I want it back. I think that western or rather industrial civilization is bound to conquer India maybe with many changes and adaptations, but none the less, in the main, based on industrialism. You have criticized strongly the many obvious defects of industrialism and hardly paid any attention to its merits. Everybody knows these defects and the utopias and social theories are meant to remove them. It is the opinion of most thinkers in the West that these defects are not due to industrialism as such but to the capitalist system which is based on exploitation of others. I believe you have stated that in your opinion there is no necessary conflict between capital and labour. I think that under the capitalist system this conflict is unavoidable.

You have advocated very eloquently and forcefully the claims of the *Daridranarayana*—the poor in India. I do believe that the remedy you have suggested is very helpful to them and if adopted by them in large number will relieve to some extent their misery. But I doubt very much if the fundamental cause of poverty are touched by it. You do not say a word against the semi-feudal zamindari system which prevails in a great part of India or against the capitalist exploitation of both the workers and the consumers.

But I must stop. I have already exceeded all reasonable limits and I hope you will forgive me. My only excuse is my mental agitation. I did not want to become the secretary of the A.I.C.C. as I wanted perfect freedom to say and do what I considered necessary. But Ansari pressed me on the ground that many of my resolutions and specially the Independence Resolution, had been passed by the Congress and I thus had full freedom to work on my own lines. I could not answer this argument and had to accept. Now, I find that every effort is being made to belittle and ridicule these very Congress resolutions and it is a painful experience.

Yours affectionately,
Jawaharlal

1. *Vide* Letter to Jawaharlal Nehru, 17-1-1928.

2.2. Letter from Jawaharlal Nehru[1]

Central Prision, Naini,
July 28, 1930

My Dear Bapuji,

It is a delight to write you again after a long interval even though it be from one prison to another. I would like to write at length, but I am afraid I cannot do so at present. I shall, therefore, confine myself to the matter in issue. Dr. Sapru and Mr. Jayakar came yesterday and had a long interview with father and me. Today they are coming again. As they have already put us in possession of all facts and shown us your note and letter, we felt we could discuss the matter between us two and arrive at some decision even without waiting for a second interview. Of course if anything new turns up at the second interview we are prepared to vary any previously-formed opinion. Our conclusions for the time being are given in the note which we are giving to Sir Tej Bahadur Sapru and Mr. Jayakar. This is more or less brief but it will, I hope, give you some idea of how our minds are working. I might add that father and I are in full agreement in regard to what our attitude should be. I might confess your point (1) regarding the constitutional issue has not won me over nor does father fancy it. I do not see how it fits in with our position or our pledges or with the realities of today. Father and I entirely agree with you that we can be "no parties to any truce which would undo the position at which we have arrived today". It is because of this that fullest consideration is essential before any final decision is arrived at. I must confess I do not see an appreciable advance yet from the other side and I greatly fear a false or weak move on our part. I am expressing myself moderately. For myself I delight in warfare. It makes me feel that I am alive. Events of the last four months in India have gladdened my heart and have made me prouder of Indian men, women and even children than I had ever been, but I realize that most people are not warlike and like peace and so I try hard to suppress myself and take a peaceful view. May I congratulate you on the new India you have created by your magic touch! What the future will bring I know not, but the past has made life worth living and our prosaic existence has developed something of epic greatness in it. Sitting here in Naini Jail I have pondered on the wonderful efficacy of non-violence as a weapon and have become a greater convert with the response of a convert to it than ever before. I hope you are not dissatisfied with the response of the country to the non-violence creed.

Despite occasional lapses, the country has stuck to it wonderfully, certainly far more grimly than I had expected. I am afraid I am still somewhat of a protestant regarding your eleven points. Not that I disagree with anyone of them. Indeed they are important. Yet I do not think that they take the place of independence. But I certainly agree with you that we should have "nothing to do with anything that would not give the nation power to give immediate effect to them". Father has been unwell the last eight days ever since he took an injection. He has grown very weak. This long interview last evening tired him out.

Jawaharlal

Please do not be anxious about me. It is only a passing trouble and I hope to get over it in two or three days. Love.

Motilal Nehru

[PS.]
We have had another talk with Sir Tej Bahadur Sapru and Mr. Jayakar. At their desire we have made some alterations in our note, but they do not make any vital difference. Our position is quite clear and I have no doubt whatever about it. I hope you will appreciate it.
The Hindu, 5-9-1930.

---

1. *Vide* "Letter to Motilal Nehru", 23-7-1930.

2.3. Letter from Jawaharlal Nehru[1]

Dehradun Jail,
May 5, 1933

My Dear Bapu,

Your letter came today. I was half expecting it for your large heart never permits you to forget anyone. I have sent you a telegram already.

As my telegram will indicate, I feel utterly at a loss and do not know what I can say to you. Religion is not familiar ground for me, and as I have grown older, I have definitely drifted away from it. I suppose, I have something else in its place, something other than just intellect, reason, which gives me strength and hope.

Apart from this undefinable and indefinite urge, which may have just a tinge of religion in it but is wholly different from it, I have grown to rely entirely on the workings of the mind. Perhaps they are weak supports to rely upon, but, search as I will, I can see no better ones. Religion seems to me to lead to emotion and sentimentality and they are still more unreliable guides. Intuition—undoubtedly there is such a thing, though where it comes from I cannot say! Perhaps from the stored up experiences at the back of the mind, the sub-conscious self.

The *Harijan* question is bad, very bad, but it seems to me incorrect to say that there is nothing so bad in all the world. I think I could point to much that was equally bad and even worse. All over the world there is this same *Harijan* question in various forms. Is it not the outcome of special causes? Surely it is due to something more than mere ignorance and ill will. To remove those causes or to neutralize their effect appears to be the only way to deal with the roots of the matter. But why should I write of these matters now! I do not want to argue in this letter as the stage for argument seems to be past.

It is hard to be so far from you, and yet it would be harder to be near you. This crowded world is a very lonely place, and you want to make it still lonelier. Life and death matter little, or should matter little. The only thing that matters is the cause that one works for, and if one could be sure that the best service to it is to die for it, then death would seem simpler. I have loved life—the mountains and the sea, the sun and rain and storm and snow, and animals, and books and art, and even human beings—and life has been good to me. But the idea of death has never frightened me, from a distance it seems fitting enough as the crown of one's endeavour. But at close quarters, it is not pleasant to contemplate.

The last fourteen or fifteen years have been a wonderful time for me, ever since I had the good fortune to be associated with you in various activities. Life became fuller and richer and more worthwhile, and that is a dear and precious memory which nothing can take from me. And whenever the future happens to be dark, this vision of the past will relieve the gloom and give strength.

All my love to you.

Yours affectionately,
Jawaharlal

[PS.]
Kamala is staying in Dehradun. I shall communicate your message to her.

---

1. *Vide* "Letter to Jawaharlal Nehru", 2-5-1933.

2.4. Letter from Jawaharlal Nehru[1]

'Parnakuti',
September 13, 1933

My Dear Bapu,

In our recent conversation you will remember that I laid stress on the reiteration and clearer definition of our national objective.

The objective of political independence has been finally laid down by the Congress and there is nothing to add to it or take away from it. We stand for complete independence. Sometimes a little confusion arises because of vague phraseology and misleading propaganda and it is therefore as well to remove this confusion by a reiteration of our political demand.

Even the word 'independence' is used with a variety of meanings. Obviously it must include, as the Congress has clearly and definitely laid down, full control of the army and of foreign relations, as well as financial and economic control.

In regard to economic matters, the Karachi Congress by passing the important resolution on "Fundamental Rights and Economic Policy" gave a lead and pointed out the direction in which we should move. I attach great importance to that resolution, but I would personally like to go much further and to clarify the position still more.

It seems to me that if we are to improve the condition of the masses, to raise them economically and give them freedom, it is inevitable that vested interests in India will have to give up their special position and many of their privileges. It is inconceivable to me how else the masses can rise. Therefore, the problem of achieving freedom becomes one of revising vested interests in favour of the masses.

To the extent this is done, to that extent only will freedom come. The biggest vested interest in India is that of the British Government; next come the Indian Princes; and others follow. We do not wish to injure any class or group and the divesting should be done as gently as possible and with every effort to avoid injury. But it is obvious that the divesting is bound to cause loss to the classes or groups which enjoy special privileges at the expense of the masses. It is also obvious that the process of divesting must be as speedy as possible to bring relief to the masses whose condition, as you know, is as bad as it can well be. Indeed economic forces themselves are acting with amazing rapidity today and breaking up the old order. The big zamindari and taluqdari system in the United Provinces has largely collapsed, though it may be kept up for some time longer by outside agencies. Even the condition of the zamindars is very bad and the peasantry of course are in a far worse position.

We are all agreed that the Round Table Conference and its various productions are utterly useless to solve even one of India's many problems. As I conceive it, the Round Table Conference was an effort to consolidate the vested interests of India behind the British Government so as to face the rising and powerful national and economic movements in the country which threaten these interests. Essentially, in international parlance, it was a fascist grouping of vested and possessing interests, and fascist methods were adopted in India to suppress the national movement. And because the mere preservation of all these vested interests in India cannot possibly solve our economic ills, whether those of the masses or even of the middle classes, the effort is foredoomed to inevitable failure. Even from the point of view of a democratic nationalism, as you yourself stated at the Round Table Conference, democracy and autocracy can ill go together.

Another aspect has to be borne in mind. The problem of Indian freedom cannot be separated from the vital international problems of the world. The present crisis in the world's affairs is having its repercussions in India. At any moment it may result in a complete breakdown or in a violent international conflagration. Everywhere there is a conflict and a contest between the forces of progress and betterment of the masses and the forces of reaction and vested interests. We cannot remain silent witnesses to this titanic struggle for it affects us intimately. Both on the narrower ground of our own interests and the wider ground of international welfare and human progress, we must, I feel, range ourselves with the progressive forces of the world.

This ranging ourselves at present can of course be ideological only. These are some of the larger issues that fill my mind and I am convinced, not only that we ignore them at our peril, but that a true appreciation of them will vitalize and give new meaning to our struggle for freedom which we must continue till the full objective is achieved.

These wider issues are of great importance but at present, as you know, the minds of large numbers of our countrymen are greatly exercised over immediate national problems and especially the question of carrying on the struggle. The statements that you and Sjt. M.S. Aney issued some time ago to guide the country have, I am afraid, produced some confusion and there has even been some resentment in regard to particular directions contained in them. There is a vague talk, in quarters which ought to know better, that the Congress has been dissolved. It is obvious that nothing of the kind has been done or could be done under the constitution. Your directions and those of Mr. Aney were, I take it, in the nature of advice or suggestions to meet a certain position that had arisen. The Congress continues as before but it is clear that it cannot function normally when Government declare its committees to be illegal. There can be no regular offices or open activity. To recognize this fact and to adapt ourselves to it is not to wind up any Congress Committee, much less the Congress organization as a whole.

A necessary consequence from this was to avoid the possibility of a few newcomers who formed committees, when the old members and other reliable workers went to prison, or even individuals, committing the Congress to an undesirable course of action. As is known, we have had to face this risk in the past and unreliable persons have come to the helm of affairs in some local areas with the intention of obstructing and even stopping the very activities they were supposed to further. It thus becomes desirable to prevent such unreliable persons from exploiting the name of the Congress Committee. This of course does not prevent Congress workers in any area from co-operating together in an organized way for the furtherance of our programme.

Confusion has also arisen in the country about the implications of individual and mass civil disobedience. I appreciate to some extent the difference but this difference does not appear to me to be a fundamental one, as, in any event, civil disobedience is essentially an individual affair. Individual civil disobedience can develop into mass civil disobedience. Besides, you told me that if an organization felt strong enough to undertake the responsibility and the risk, it could, of its own initiative, take up mass civil disobedience. Indeed you were of opinion that a local organization could, in this manner go ahead in any direction which was not contrary to Congress methods or policy.

Stress was laid in your previous statement on the undesirability of secrecy, although you pointed out that there was nothing inherently illegitimate in secret methods. I think that most of us agree, and certainly I am of that opinion, that our movement is essentially an open one and secret methods do not fit in with it. Such methods, if indulged in to any large extent, are likely to change the whole character of the movement, as it has been conceived, and produce a certain amount of demoralization. Agreeing with this, some of us feel that, to some extent as for instance in communicating with each other or sending directions or keeping contacts, a measure of secrecy may be necessary. Perhaps secrecy is hardly the word for those activities and privacy would suit them better. Privacy of course is always open to all groups and individuals. Secrecy or the avoidance of it, as you said, cannot be made into a fetish.

But secrecy is certainly involved in the production of printed or duplicated news-sheets and bulletins. These bulletins have often served a useful purpose in the past in keeping contact between headquarters and districts and in sending information or directions. You pointed out to me the difficulties and undesirable consequences of running these secret presses and duplicating machines. Many good workers are tied up and have to avoid aggressive action; money has to be invested in such machines and frequently they are taken away by the police. Even from the practical point of view this continuous drain and tying up of workers is not desirable, and undoubtedly it sometimes results in demoralization. You suggested that the best way was to have handwritten copies of bulletins, etc., containing the name of the publisher. Generally, I agree with all this and appreciate the force of your argument. But I do feel that under certain circumstances it may be desirable for a local or Provincial committee or group to issue bulletins of directions, etc., secretly. This must not be encouraged; indeed it should be discouraged, but a certain latitude in exceptional circumstances might be permitted.

There is one other small matter which seems to me rather ridiculous. It was right and proper, if I may say so, for you to court imprisonment by giving previous intimation of your intention to do so to the authorities. But it seems to me to be perfectly absurd for others, and even Congress volunteers, to send such notices or communications to the authorities. Any person desiring to offer civil resistance should openly carry on activities which further our cause and thus court arrest. He must not forget or ignore these activities and merely ask to be arrested.

This letter has become long enough. I do not mention here the many other matters which I had the privilege of discussing with you.

Yours affectionately,
Jawahar

Mahatma Gandhi
Poona

Bombay Secret Abstracts, Home Department, Special Branch , File No. 800(40) (11)-C; also *Mahatma,* Vol. III, pp. 305-308.

---

1. *Vide* "Letter to Jawaharlal Nehru", 14-9-1933.

2.5. Letter from Jawaharlal Nehru[1]

Anand Bhawan, Allahabad,
August 13, 1934

My Dear Bapu,

After just six months of absolute seclusion and little exercise I have felt rather lost in the anxiety, excitement and activity of the past 27 hours. I feel very tired. I am writing this letter to you at midnight. All day there have been crowds of people coming. If I have the chance I shall write to you again, but I doubt if I shall be able to do so for some months. I am, therefore, going to indicate to you briefly how I have reacted to the various major Congress decisions of the last five months or so.

My sources of information have naturally been strictly limited but I think that they were sufficient to enable me to form a fairly correct idea of the general trend of events.

When I heard that you had called off the C.D. movement I felt unhappy.

Only the brief announcement reached me at first. Much later I read your statement and this gave me one of the biggest shocks I have ever had. I was prepared to reconcile myself to the withdrawal of C.D. But the reasons you gave for doing so and the suggestions you made for future work astounded me. I had a sudden and intense feeling, that something broke inside me, a bond that I had valued very greatly had snapped. I felt terribly lonely in this wide world. I have always felt a little lonely almost from childhood up. But a few bonds strengthened me, a few strong supports held me up. That loneliness never went, but it was lessened. But now I felt absolutely alone, left high and dry on a desert island.

Human beings have an enormous capacity for adapting themselves and so I too adapted myself to some extent to the new conditions. The keenness of my feelings on the subject, which amounted almost to physical pain, passed off; the edge was dulled. But shock after shock, a succession of events sharpened that edge to a fine point, and allowed my mind or feelings no peace or rest. Again I felt that sensation of spiritual isolation, of being a perfect stranger out of harmony, not only with the crowds that passed me, but also with those whom I had valued as dear and close comrades. My stay in prison this time became a greater ordeal for my nerves than any previous visit had been. I almost wished that all newspapers might be kept away from me so that I might be spared these repeated shocks.

Physically, I kept fairly well. I always do in prison. My body has served me well and can stand a great deal of ill-treatment and strain. And being vain enough to imagine that perhaps I might yet do some effective work in this land to which fate had tied me, I looked after it well.

But I wondered often enough if I was not a square peg in a round hole, or a bubble of conceit thrown about hither and thither on an ocean which spurned me. But vanity and conceit triumphed and the intellectual apparatus that functions within me refused to admit defeat. If the ideals that had spurred me to action and had kept me buoyed up through stormy weather were right—and the conviction of their rightness ever grew within me—they were bound to triumph though my generation might not live to witness that triumph.

But what had happened to those ideals during these long and weary months of this year when I was a silent and distant witness, fretting at my helplessness?

Setbacks and temporary defeats are common enough in all great struggles. They grieve but one recovers soon enough. One recovers soon if the light of those ideals is not allowed to grow dim and the anchor of principles holds fast. But what I saw was not setback and defeat but that spiritual defeat which is the most terrible of all. Do not imagine that I am referring to the council-entry question. I do not attach vital importance to it. Under certain circumstances I can even imagine entering a legislature myself. But whether I function inside or outside the legislature I function as a revolutionary, meaning thereby a person working for the fundamental and revolutionary changes, political and social, for I am convinced that no other changes can bring peace or satisfaction to India and the world.

So I thought. Not so evidently the leaders who were functioning outside.

They began to talk the language of an age gone by before the heady wine of N.C.O. and C.D. had fired our heads. Sometimes they used the same words and phrases but they were dead words without life or real meaning. The leading figures of the Congress suddenly became those people who had obstructed us, held us back, kept aloof from the struggle and even co-operated with the opposite party in the time of our direct need. They became the high priests in our temple of freedom and many a brave soldier who had shouldered the burden in the heat and dust of the fray was not even allowed inside the temple precincts. He had many like him had become untouchables and unapproachables. And if he ventured to raise his voice and criticize the new high priests, he was shouted down and to[l] that he was a traitor to the cause because he spoilt the harmony of the sacred precincts.

And so the flag of Indian freedom was entrusted with all pomp and circumstance to those who had actually hauled it down at the height of our national struggle at the bidding of the enemy; to those who had proclaimed from the housetops that they had given up politics—for politics were unsafe then—but who emerged with a jump to the front ranks when politics became safe.

And what of the ideals they set forth before them, speaking as they did on behalf of the Congress and the nation? A pitiful hotch-potch, avoiding real issues, toning down, as far as they dared, even the political objective of the Congress, expressing a tender solicitude for every vested interest, bowing down to many a declared enemy of freedom, but showing great truculence and courage in facing the advanced and fighting elements in the Congress ranks. Is not the Congress being rapidly reduced to a magnified edition of that shameful spectacle, the Calcutta Corporation during the last few years? Might not the dominant part of the Bengal Congress be called today "the society for the advancement of Mr. Nalini Ranjan Sirkar", a gentleman who rejoiced to entertain Government officials, Home Members and the like, when most of us were in prison and C.D. was supposed to be flourishing—And the other part probably a similar society for a similar laudable object? But the fault does not lie with Bengal alone. Almost everywhere there is a similar outlook. The Congress from top to bottom is a caucus and opportunism triumphs.

The Working Committee is not directly responsible for this state of affairs. But nonetheless the Working Committee must shoulder the responsibility. It is the leaders and their policy that shape the activities of the followers. It is neither fair nor just to throw blame on the followers. Every language has some saying about the workman blaming his tools. The committee had deliberately encouraged vagueness in the definition of our ideals and objectives and this is bound to lead not only to confusion but to demoralization during periods of reaction, and to the emergence of the demagogue and the reactionary.

I am referring especially to the political objectives which are the special province of the Congress. I feel that the time is overdue for the Congress to think clearly on social and economic issues but I recognize that education on these issues takes time and the Congress as a whole may not be able to go as far at present as I would like it to. But it appears that whether the Working Committee knows anything about the subject or not it is perfectly willing to denounce and to excommunicate people who happen to have made a special study of the subject and hold certain views.

No attempt is made to understand those views, which, it is notorious, are held by a very large number of the ablest and most self-sacrificing people in the world. Those views may be right or wrong but they deserve at least some understanding before the Working Committee sets out to denounce them. It is hardly becoming for a reasoned argument to be answered by sentimental appeals or by the cheap remark that the condition in India are different and the economic laws that apply elsewhere do not function here. The resolution of the Working Committee on the subject showed such an astounding ignorance of the elements of socialism that it was painful to read it and to realize that it might be read outside India. It seemed that the overmastering desire of the Committee was somehow to assure various vested interests even at the risk of talking nonsense.

A strange way of dealing with the subject of socialism is to use the word, which has a clearly defined meaning in the English language, in a totally different sense. For individuals to use words in a sense peculiar to themselves is not helpful in the commerce of ideas. A person who declares himself to be an engine-driver and then adds that his engine is of wood and is drawn by bullocks is misusing the word engine driver.

This letter has become a much longer one than I expected and the night is already far spent. Probably I have written in a confused and scrappy way for my brain is tired. But still it will convey some picture of my mind. The last few months have been very painful ones for me and, I take it, for many others. I have felt sometimes that in the modern world, and perhaps in the ancient world also, it is oft preferred to break some people's hearts rather than touch other's pockets. Pockets are indeed valuable and more cherished than hearts and brains and bodies and human justice and dignity.

There is one other subject I should like to mention. That is the Swaraj Bhawan Trust. I understand that the Working Committee recently considered the question of the unkeep of the Swaraj Bhawan and came to the conclusion that it was not responsible for it. As however, it had already made a grant about three years ago and this had not been paid yet, although expenses were incurred on the strength of it, a fresh grant was sanctioned. This will probably be enough for some months. In regard to the future, the Working Committee was evidently anxious not to be saddled with the burden of maintaining the house and grounds. This burden amounts to Rs. 100 a month, which includes taxes, etc. The trustees, I understand, were also a little frightened of the burden and suggested that parts of the house might be let in the ordinary way to raise money for the maintenance. Another suggestion was made that part of the grounds might be sold off for this purpose. I was surprised to learn of these suggestions, as some of them seemed to me to be contrary to the letter of the trust and all of them against its spirit. As an individual trustee I have only one voice in the matter but I should like to say that I have the strongest possible objection to any such misuse of the trust property. The very idea of the wishes of my father being flouted in this way is intolerable to me. The trust represented not only his wishes but also in small way a memorial to him and his wishes and his memory is dearer to me than a hundred rupees a month. I should, therefore, like to assure the Working Committee and the trustees that they need have no anxiety on the score of the money required for maintenance of the property. As soon as the funds, now granted by the Working Committee for some months, are exhausted, I shall make myself personally responsible for the maintenance and no further grant need be made by the Working Committee. I would also beg the trustees to respect my feelings in this matter and not to break-up the property or to hire it for the sake of hiring it out. I shall endeavour to maintain the Swaraj Bhawan property till such time as it is put to some worthy use.

I have not the figures by me but I believe that even thus far the Swaraj Bhawan has not been, in any sense, a financial burden on the Working Committee. The grants that have been paid to it will probably not be much in excess of reasonable rent for the quarters occupied by the office of the A.I.C.C. This rent could have been reduced by occupying smaller and cheaper quarters. At the same time in the past the A.I.C.C. has paid as much as Rs. 150 a month for rent of an upper floor only in Madras.

Perhaps some part of this letter might pain you. But you would not have me hide my heart from you.

Yours affectionately,
Jawahar

[PS.]
I received your short note in Alipore Jail and I sent an answer. But the Superintendent suppressed that answer.

A Bunch of Old Letters, pp. 112-17.

---

1. *Vide* "Letter to Jawaharlal Nehru", 17-8-1934 and "Letter to Vallabhbhai Patel", 19-8-1934.

2.6. Letter from Jawaharlal Nehru[1]

May 25, 1936

About women and W.C. I began by saying that I had received some protests for their non-inclusion. I would have welcomed even stronger protests for I wanted our women to be more aggressive and to insist on their rights, both political and social. I invited them to organize themselves to press for their rights which they were not likely to get if they waited for the goodwill of their menfolk. About the W.C. I said that it was formed under peculiar circumstances when I had to play an unusual part. The *hayadar* (self-respecting) president would probably have resigned and I being *behaya* (shameless) stuck on even though the majority of the Congress had decided against me on some vital issues. This peculiar position was reflected in the formation of the W.C., which certainly could not be under the circumstances of my choice although technically I was responsible for it. When various viewpoints have to be represented, the lesser ones go to the wall. You are perfectly right in saying that I was responsible for the exclusion of women. But yet this is not the whole matter. I would have liked to have a woman in the Working Committee but as the matters developed and a number of other names appeared and stayed, there was little choice left. Ultimately I felt that it mattered little to me who was in the W.C. and who was not. The Committee as it took shape was not my child, I could hardly recognize it and to some inclusions, as you know, I reacted strongly. Yet ultimately I submitted but inevitably with the thought that I was surrendering to others and almost against my own better judgement. At the very first meeting, almost without provocations, the inherent conflicts appeared. The whole purpose of a president nominating a homogeneous committee was thus frustrated.

---

1. *Vide* "Letter to Narandas Gandhi", 27-9-1935.

2.7. Letter from Jawaharlal Nehru[1]

November 14, 1937

My Dear Bapu,

I have just read your article on the A.I.C.C. meeting. Regarding the Mysore resolution you have said that it was *ultra vires* of the A.I.C.C. If this was so then I had no business to permit discussion on it and should have banned it. I am not aware of any constitutional provision which leads to this result and only something in the nature of such a provision can bar a resolution moved in the ordinary way and supported by a majority of the A.I.C.C. Apart from the constitution itself, I am not aware of any previous decision of the Congress or the A.I.C.C. which lays down that such matters should not be considered. Even if there was some such resolution, I do not see how it could prevent the A.I.C.C. from considering a matter if it so chose, unless the resolution was embodied in a rule of practice. The A.I.C.C. is at complete liberty to consider a resolution which may go contrary to a previous resolution passed by itself. If however, there is a rule of practice or procedure, this has to be acted upon till the A.I.C.C. does not alter it [*sic.*]. There is no question of such a rule, but I do not even know of a resolution which lays down a policy which the Mysore resolution infringes. In statements issued by us in the past mention has been made that the Congress desires to follow a policy of non-intervention in the States.

Those statements cannot bar the A.I.C.C. itself from intervening if it chooses. I cannot understand how the legal phrase, *ultra vires*, can be made to apply.

Another question arises, what is intervention? Is a mention of a State in a resolution intervention? Is a demand for civil liberties or a condemnation of repression, intervention? If so, the Congress itself has been guilty of it in specific and unequivocal terms during the last two years.

The Mysore resolution of the A.I.C.C. is very badly worded and, in any event, I did not want it to be passed by the A.I.C.C. just then. But my feelings have little to do with the matter. I have to act as the president of a democratic assembly.

The resolution was one of condemnation of repression in Mysore. Are we to refrain from condemning repression in a State in future whatever the nature of this repression? If this repression consists in attacking the Congress itself, insulting our Flag, or banning our organization, are we to remain silent? These matters must be cleared up so that our office and our organization might know definitely what line we are to take up.

You have said that the A.I.C.C. should not have passed the resolution without at least hearing the other side. Do you think that it is feasible for us to appoint inquiry committees to go to States? Will the States agree? on several occasions I have suggested this to States—not a committee but just an individual to go there and inquire from both sides. They have invariably turned this down.

This Mysore matter has been going on for a long time. The Karnatak P.C.C. has taken some steps in the matter. Their secretary has had a long interview with the Dewan of Mysore. I have repeatedly written to the Dewan and put a large number of specific cases before him. He has replied at length without, in my opinion, justifying the State policy. For months past I have been restraining Congressmen in Mysore from indulging in any disobedience of orders and, in fact, no orders have been disobeyed, except by Nariman recently. The Karnatak P.C.C. ultimately considered the situation and condemned the policy of repression in Mysore and asked us for further directions as to what they should do. It is hardly correct therefore to say that the A.I.C.C. condemned anybody unheard or *ex parte*. We pursued all the ordinary avenues open to us.

I am writing all this to you as I want to be clear in my own mind what our policy is. You have censured the A.I.C.C. and me for the course we pursued. I have not yet understood how and where I am wrong and so long as I do not understand it, I can hardly act otherwise.

Yours affectionately,
Jawaharlal

Mahatma Gandhi
Wardha (C.P.)

A Bunch of Old Letters, pp. 254-56

1. *Vide* "The A.I.C.C.", 13-11-1937.

2.8. Letter from Jawaharlal Nehru[1]

August 10, 1940

My Dear Bapu,

I have just received your letter of the 8th. About Hyderabad, I can make no suggestion. So much depends on the strength of the people and their organization. I think, however, that it is far better for them to concentrate on the rural areas where the chances of communal clashes are probably less. I do not see how they can remain passive under the circumstances. Yet it may be perhaps better not to precipitate a big crisis immediately in view of the rapid developments of the political situation in India as a whole. When this all-India situation advances further, Hyderabad people might b in a better position to assert their right.

In a sense I am not sorry at the development in Hyderabad. The impossible attitude that Bahadur Yar Khan and others have taken up will react on them. It may of course lead to a great deal of trouble and bloodshed. In any event the State Congress people should make it perfectly clear that they cannot reduce by an iota their demand for responsible government.

I understand the Working Committee is likely to meet in Wardha in eight or nine days' time. I hope to meet you then.

About the exactions for war funds. I have written to the secretary of the U.P.P.C.C. to send you some particulars. Some have been published in the Press and are clear enough. Some others, though equally clear, might be explained differently. For instance an usual case is for a person to be approached for a donation. He refuses or offers a smaller sum than what is demanded. Immediately or a day or two after, he is arrested on the charge of preventing others from subscribing to the war funds, and thereby coming in the way of war efforts.

I have just had a case like this from Allahabad district. A poor village shopkeeper was asked to give Rs. 15 or Rs. 20. He said the most he could possibly give was Rs. 5. He was cursed and sworn at and immediately a notice was given to him to appear to show cause why he should not be proceeded against under the Defence of India rules. His case is up today in a court here. Usually, this kind of thing is not done with full-fledged Congressmen who are expected to refuse anyhow. Another case which has come to me today is from Kasganj in Etah district. A Naib Tahsildar went to the shop of a Congressman on 2nd of August and demanded money for the war funds.

This was refused and the man stated that as a Congressman he could not do so. Thereupon the Naib Tahsildar threatened to take action and had the name of the person noted down. On the next day this man, who is the nephew of a well-known Congressman in the district, was suddenly arrested for non-payment of a punitive police tax. He was put in the lock-up and for 30 hours he was not given any food or facilities for bathing etc. This arrest was completely illegal as punitive tax can only be recovered by attachment of property and the person concerned, whose name is Omprakash, has considerable movable and immovable property. The amount of Punitive Tax concerned was only Rs. 6 which could easily have been realized by attachment. Omprakash's uncle, Manpal Gupta, thereupon created a lot of fuss and ultimately Omprakash was discharged. That is how the matter stands now.

Another interesting case is that of Thakur Surendra Bahadur Singh, Taluqadar of Simri in Rae Bareli district. He is a Congress M.L.A. His father, the Taluqadar, recently died and thereupon, at his own request, his taluqa was taken under the Court or Wards. The Deputy Commissioner informed him that he should contribute Rs. 1,500 to the War Fund. He refused to do so as a Congressman. He was then told that he held his taluqa on conditions of loyalty and good service and the Court of Wards had a perfect right to give the donation out of the revenues of the taluqa. Thereupon, he sent a registered notice to the Deputy Commissioner protesting against this imposition and saying that it was wholly illegal. His case was that it might or might not be open to the Government to confiscate his taluqa for want of loyalty to them. But it was certainly not open to them to give a donation on his behalf and against his will. In spite of this the Deputy Commissioner has already or is going to pay this sum to the war fund and Surendra Bahadur Singh is thinking of bringing a declaratory suit in a court of law.

I am getting complaints from various districts of pressure being brought on kisans to pay eight annas or a rupee or more per plough. It is obvious that they do not want to pay but are compelled to do so.

Petty Government servants and minor officials dare not say no when they are asked to contribute. A recent case which came to my notice informally but nevertheless correctly was that of stenotypist of a District Magistrate. He was asked to give Rs. 200. His salary was Rs. 125 a month. He pointed out hesitatingly that he had a large family and it was entirely beyond his capacity to pay that sum. He was then told that in any event he and his family would have to starve if the British lost the war. So, this was a kind of insurance that he had to pay. Ultimately, it was settled that he should pay Rs. 150 to the war fund. A curious thing is that one does not hear very much about donations from higher officials. They think it is enough for them to serve the cause by giving their very efficient service at a high rate of payment.

That number of new appointments at high salaries grows from day-to-day. Probably, a very large proportion of the funds that are being collected goes towards the payment of these high salaries. Simla, I understand, is crowded with this type of officials serving the great cause by drawing a fancy salary for little or no work. There was a recent case of an English official who was till recently drawing Rs. 750 a month suddenly being pushed into some war work and is being given Rs. 2,500 a month. It was stated that he had accepted this new job at considerable sacrifice to himself.

Yours affectionately,
Jawaharlal

Mahatma Gandhi

Gandhi-Nehru Papers, 1940. *Courtesy*: Nehru Memorial Museum and Library.

---

1. *Vide* "Letter to Lord Linlithgow", 27-8-1940.

2.9. Letter from Jawaharlal Nehru[1]

Anand Bhavan, Allahabad,
October 2, 1940

My Dear Bapu,

About six weeks ago, when I was in Bombay for the Planning Committee, I had a remarkable experience, which has oppressed me often since then. I should have told you about it when you were in Bombay last but the Working Committee and the A.I.C.C. filled my mind and I forgot. I did not want to write about it through the post.

I came back from the Planning Committee during the midday interval for food. I had to go back soon after and was pressed for time. Just then a young English boy turned up at my sister's flat. He was dressed in *khadi*—a shirt and loose *pyjamas* and [a] cap. He told me that he was an officer in the army—a Second Lieutenant—and had decided to leave the army and face the consequences. He produced a copy of a document which he said he had given to his

Commanding Officer and which had been forwarded to Army Headquarters at Simla. I read this and was amazed. It was a very fine statement. I enclose a copy of it and you can read it for yourself.

His name was Napier. He was the great grandson of the Napier who is said to have conquered Sind. The family since then had been intimately connected with the army. Apparently it came down in the world. Young Napier joined as a private a few years before the war began. But because he was a bright lad, and possibly also because of his family, he got a scholarship for Sandhurst and later became a commissioned officer. He was sent with his regiment to India a month or two after the war began. He was stationed at Mhow in Central India. Evidently he did not fit in with his brother officers. He was more serious and intellectual and he felt drawn towards India, especially to the poorer classes. He avoided officers' messes and spent his time in the bazaar or elsewhere talking to paltry shopkeepers, labourers, etc. He tried to pick up Hindustani. I think he gave a good part of his salary to the poor.

This was not liked by his brother officers. The Commanding Officer spoke to him about it and they had many arguments. He began to dislike his profession, and especially service in India, more and more. He wanted to leave it but this was not possible in war time. Ultimately, he gave the enclosed note to his C.O. His regiment was transferred from Mhow to Jhansi. This gave him a day and a half or two to join up at Jhansi. He decided to burn his boats whatever the consequences and went and sold his uniform. This was done chiefly to put a definite end to his military career—also to raise some money. He did not, particularly, want to be sent back from India to England.

He then telephoned to Allahabad to get into touch with me and learnt— found—I was in Bombay and got my address; went straight to Bombay and to my sister's house from the station.

This was a novel situation for me and I was completely taken aback. My heart went out to this young and terribly sincere boy of 25 but I did not know what to do.

By coming to Bombay he had deserted—and that too in war time. This is the gravest offence in military law and there was no doubt that he would be arrested in a day or two and court-martialled. I found from him that he was due to report at Jhansi the next morning. There was just a chance of his getting back to Jhansi in time if he took the next train which left soon after.

I wanted to have a much longer talk with Napier but already I had kept the Planning Committee waiting. If he had to go back to Jhansi by the next train then there was going to be no other chance. I felt he must go back. To be charged with desertion was to confuse the issue apart from other consequences. He had already made his position perfectly clear to the army authorities and he could face them and fight them on that issue. I could hardly conceive of his remaining in the British Army after his declaration of faith. Nor could I see how he was to get out of it. Army authorities do not permit this kind of thing. What was going to happen to him I could not guess, but it seemed to be clear that he would have a very hard time. Anyway I felt that this question must not be mixed up with desertion. I advised him, therefore, to go back by the next train to Jhansi and to report himself to the C.O. there. I further suggested to him not to do so in *khadi kurta* and *pyjamas*. He said he had shorts, etc., and he would wear them. I asked him if he had enough money. He said he had quite enough for his purpose.

He accepted my advice and said he would go back. I asked him to communicate with me, if possible, or with my sister, and to let me know what happened. We have had no news of him since. I am told now that every regiment that is sent to Jhansi, goes off soon after to Egypt. I am trying to find out now what had happened to Napier's regiment. It is quite likely that because of his views and his escapade he was kept under arrest and prevented from communicating, and later sent out of India.

His face haunts me and I often wonder if I advised him rightly.

Yours affectionately,
Jawaharlal

[Enclosure—Napier's Note]

August 1940

Having regard to the fact that the country is at war and it is not possible for an officer to resign his commission in the normal manner I here under at the request of my Commanding Officer set down my considered opinions, in the belief that these are incompatible with the retention of my commission. I am infinitely more proud of these opinions than of the fact that my family has an unbroken tradition of service in the British Army for the past

150 years, and that one of my forbears played no small part in conquering India.

I am opposed to British Rule in India. I consider that a country should be ruled by its inhabitants, because freedom is the most important thing of all. It is even more important than food, but food is also important. In India no one has freedom, and a large proportion of the population have insufficient food, a fact plainly evident to any Englishman who took the trouble to miss his drinks at the club for one evening and go into the country to look.

I am opposed to the British Empire. I consider it to be an association for the making of money, propagated by merchants in England under a hypothetical screen of "Empire glory and the betterment of the native races". I consider this bad for the majority of people in England, bad for India, and bad for the world. There is this much difference between Hitlerism and Bolshevism on the one hand and British Imperialism on the other. The latter gives liberty and food to some and neither to others. The former gives food to all and liberty to none. I am opposed to modern European civilization, which is the grandiose name under which the present mess in the vicinity of the North Sea is known. I find it difficult to believe that the peoples at present engaged in a mad struggle generated by greed and fear are a force for good in the world. European civilization has produced the means for making things, and rather more efficiently the means for destroying what it has made. Its most important effect on the mind of the ordinary man is that it has produced an inability to think, and a distrust of those who can. It is seen at its best in war time, when everyone has work and money, and is reasonably happy in the pursuit of killing his fellow men. In peace time, there is unemployment, starvation and misery. Surely even an Englishman can see something wrong there.

I am opposed to the Englishman as a means of spreading culture and civilization. The average Englishman values his body to such an extent that he neglects his mind. Certainly the body should be fit, and be exercised to be fit, but why do people assume that the mind needs no exercise. An effete mind in a healthy body is a matter for satisfaction to an Englishman, whereas an active mind in a feeble body is a thing of contempt to him. English ideas of life are with few exceptions based on this principle, which is in direct opposition to the Oriental view of life. I cannot willingly help the English to propagate suet-headed mentality. And for the third part of man, that elusive thing called soul! The average Englishman neglects this completely. The English are an irreligious people. The lower classes make no bones about this; on the other hand the higher classes treat religion as a social function. By a mixture of hypocrisy and sheer stupidity they manage to convince themselves they are Christians, though in practice they utterly disregard the magnificent precepts of their religion, and if Christ were to appear today in England, they would regard him as a most undesirable fellow. One point of the Christian religion is to pray daily. You who read this, do you pray daily? Would you kneel down in a public place and pray to your God? Yet Indians do this everyday. I am not religious myself, a fact which I consider a cause for regret. I am not a Christian, but neither do I pretend to be one. Despite this I deplore my unacceptability in the eyes of my Commanding Officer, a thing which no decent Englishman would do, be he Christian or no. Nor do I in spite of my irreligion scoff at the beliefs of others, whose ignorance and superstition at the present time is due to a Government which so far from teaching them anything, has in a hundred and fifty years made no attempt to see that they have sufficient to eat. I have as much sympathy with the Hindu religion as with the Christian, and infinitely more with the Indian people than with the British.

Few Europeans object to the British themselves, but most of them object to their hypocrisy, which allows them to feather their nests at the expense of all and sundry while believing themselves in a muddled sort of way to be the saviours of mankind.

Few Indians like the British or their rule. This applies equally inside the Cantonments as outside them. The people whose work depends on the British keep their opinions to themselves, but outside the Cantonments any man who is not in receipt of a Government pension will very gladly say what his opinions are. As to the opinion of Indians in the Army, particularly those commissioned, I leave it for someone sufficiently painstaking to find out. Considering that the state of the average Englishman in such matters is such that after thirty years in the country he can with difficulty speak the language, there seems little chance of this happening.

But it is quite an important question; and the answer is not merely 'Yes' or 'No'. In India all questions have several answers.

Finally, I must assert that I am not taking this course without due consideration, nor was it on the spur of the moment that I suggested to my Commanding Officer that it might be better if I left the Army. I have a good position; pay that is roughly twice my requirements (thanks to the munificence of the Government at the cost of a population who need it far more than myself), in addition to a scholarship obtained with some labour at the Royal Military College. I am now prepared to leave that, to leave a profession in which I have always been keen, and to cut myself off from such friends and relations as I have in England. 'Prepared' is not the right word. 'Hoping' would be more appropriate. I do this against the advice of every Indian in the *bazar*, who assures me that though he would certainly prefer an *Indian* Government to a British one, he has no intention of doing anything about it, since his livelihood depends on the British. I am well aware that anything I may do will make scarcely a ripple in an ocean which at the present time is as near to being churned with blood as ever before. But if one must join in the general fight in this mad world, it is surely a feeble creature who would not fight for what he believes to be right, even if he must do it without a bank balance. Freedom is more important than food.

1. *Vide* "Letter to Jawaharlal Nehru", 6-10-1940.

Subject Index

Subject Index